PEACEFUL
MONTESSORI
PARENTING

PEACEFUL MONTESSORI PARENTING

A Guide to Raising Capable Kids with Joy, Simplicity, and Intention

HALEY TURNER
of kindly.HALEY

QUARRY

Quarto.com

© 2025 Quarto Publishing Group USA Inc.
Text, Photos © 2025 Haley Turner

First Published in 2025 by Quarry Books, an imprint of The Quarto Group,
100 Cummings Center, Suite 265-D, Beverly, MA 01915, USA.
T (978) 282-9590 F (978) 283-2742

Quarry Books titles are also available at discount for retail, wholesale, promotional, and bulk purchase. For details, contact the Special Sales Manager by email at specialsales@quarto.com or by mail at The Quarto Group, Attn: Special Sales Manager, 100 Cummings Center, Suite 265-D, Beverly, MA 01915, USA.

10 9 8 7 6 5 4 3 2 1

ISBN: 978-0-7603-9008-5

Digital edition published in 2025
eISBN: 978-0-7603-9009-2

Library of Congress Cataloging-in-Publication Data is available.

Page Design: Cindy Samargia Laun
Cover Illustration: Zoe Naylor and Jessica Maher
Illustration: Zoe Naylor, Jessica Maher, and Shutterstock

Printed in China

Dedication

To my husband and our babies.

You are the dream I've always dreamt.
I love growing alongside you.

Forever <3

contents

introduction

Welcome to the world of peaceful Montessori parenting, your heartfelt guide to navigating the incredible journey of raising capable, thriving little humans.

This book brings the age-old wisdom of Montessori and the modern-day research of peaceful parenting into our lives, offering clarity and ease in real-life, everyday situations. From navigating tricky behaviors with calm and intention, to setting up an environment that fosters independence, to understanding your child's unique needs—you'll feel supported all around in your parenting journey.

8

Who Is This Book For?

This book is for all parents, caregivers, and anyone interested in fostering a conscious Montessori lifestyle. Whether you're a first-time parent or have multiple children, are a caregiver responsible for children's well-being and education, or are someone eager to support friends and family in raising children, this guide is for you.

Navigating the Book

Keeping in mind that all of us parents of young children are often running on suboptimal sleep, busy schedules, and the balancing act of a lifetime—I wanted to be sure that this is a super easy to navigate book for you! It's organized into four main parts:

- Part 1: The Guide: Understanding your crucial role in your child's development.

- Part 2: The Child: Insights into your child's journey and needs.

- Part 3: The Environment: Creating an ideal and realistic environment for learning and growth.

- Part 4: The Work: Exploring why, how, and when to offer Montessori-inspired activities.

Throughout the book, you'll find Montessori-inspired activities to bring all your learning into day-to-day life with your little ones. To take all the guesswork out of it, you have a clear guide, as described here, on what will be appropriate for your child's age, development, and interests.

These activities are meant to be as easy as absolutely possible for you, while also being a big benefit to the child. Remember, you can fully embrace these Montessori principles and your child can thrive within them, even if you are working full-time, you're not crafty, and have never used a glue gun—because it's about so much more than just this!

if	when	then
"If you notice" focuses on: -Child's Interest -Developmental needs -Behavioral challenges -Observations -Etc	*"When?"* focuses on: - Child's age - Developmental stage - Ideal times of day - Etc	*"Then* offer this to" focuses on: - Goals -Objectives -Benefits -Etc

This book and your peaceful Montessori parenting journey are more than just principles and practices; they're a celebration of the parent–child relationship. It's a reminder of the small triumphs, the shared laughter, and the tender moments of connection. Through storytelling, practical guidance, and a heartfelt invitation to self-discovery, you'll feel empowered to embrace parenthood as a beautiful adventure, where love, respect, and understanding pave the way for generations to come.

A Note to Parents
Let's get started by chatting about what really matters—my favorite kind of chat, the kind where we skip the small talk and get to the heart of things. Imagine that you and I meet up at a coffee shop. We've got some time to ourselves, no kids in tow, and we can have a real conversation. We ask how one another is doing, exchanging friendly niceties. You say, "I'm doing fine." And I smile, nod, and say the same.

We sit in silence for a moment and then, in unison, we both say, "How are you doing, *really?*"

There are few things in life like that friend who genuinely cares; who truly wants to help; who can see through a façade. The type of person you can lean on. And to be honest, in our modern and busy world, the village we all expected isn't always there. Generational

wisdom on raising kids, raising ourselves, and thriving in our new family unit somehow seems more lacking than ever before. Even for the lucky ones with support from those who have already walked this path, it's just such a different world today.

We all have so very much to learn—myself included.

Raising kids is hard and we're all doing the very best we can. So, before we go any further into this thing, let's take a moment to pause. Breathe. Put your hand on your heart and say out loud, "I'm an amazing parent. I'm exactly the parent my child needs." Because you are. After over a decade in the field of early childhood education and development, having worked with families all over the world, and truly being dedicated to this work—I still don't always get it "right" and that's okay. One thing I'm sure of is that it's most often the *good* parents who find parenting difficult. It's most often the *good* parents who wonder if they've done enough for their kids. As you cozy in to read this book, picking it up here and there when you have a few moments, please know it's an incredibly *good* parent who seeks further education and support on raising kids. And look at you, reading this book. There are kids all around the world, grown-ups, eighty-year-olds, even, who all wish their parents took the time to read, grow, learn, and heal. You are doing that. You are amazing.

9

My greatest intention in writing this book is that it serves as a light when you're worn out, stressed, and feeling a bit (or very) lost. Every parent deserves to reflect on their tough days and think, "Hmm, that was really hard *and* I know what shifts I can make for tomorrow to support myself and my family better. It won't stay this hard forever, because I have the tools."

We'll honor our past selves, embrace the present, and hold the promise of a brighter future for our children and ourselves—it just takes some work to grow into the parent we want to show up as.

It makes so much sense that we've seen the Montessori movement pick up even more interest in the 21st century, as it continues to flood our internet world and fill our hearts with guidance and support. For many, it serves as an anchor as we grasp for some consistency, simplicity, and certainty amongst the beautiful chaos of raising kids in a modern world.

To emphasize just how much this philosophy means to me, I'll stay true to my word, skipping the small talk to share a bit of how I ended up writing this book for you.

In my first year of classroom teaching, as an excited twenty-two-year-old, I was diagnosed with a rare brain condition and underwent brain and spinal surgery. After surprising complications and a year of physical therapy to relearn how to walk properly and simply function, my doctors and I realized that returning to the classroom was no longer an option. My life took such an unexpected turn, and as someone who felt certain of my passion and purpose as a teacher, it was all very difficult to process. Desperately clinging to life before my diagnosis, I found myself immersed in Dr. Montessori's work, seeking to align her principles of honoring every unique human with my own challenging journey. Having done my student teaching in a Montessori school, I was familiar with and interested in this work—but it wasn't until life closed one door that the Montessori window truly opened for me. Her work helped me find a way to accept and embrace myself, once again respecting my own body and needs, while still living out my purpose. It was then that I realized the Montessori approach is so much more than pedagogy. Thus, my own Montessori lifestyle began!

Once I completed my Montessori accreditations, I began working in homes, consulting, nannying, guiding homeschoolers, and coaching parents through their parenting challenges. I pursued further certifications, training, and personal growth, culminating in a unique perspective that I hope you'll feel throughout my words here. As I worked alongside these wonderful families, though, I came to realize that what many perceived as the "Montessori Method" at home was reduced to expensive wooden toys, meticulously organized and aesthetic playrooms, extravagant baby gear, and a relentless stream of activities to keep children entertained at all times. This all felt inaccessible, inaccurate, and unfair to parents—and to the children, most of all! I could see the beautiful depth of a Montessori lifestyle that, in a lot of ways, saved me, were lost to many.

Some years later, I became a mother to a sweet baby girl, and found myself sitting in our tiny city townhouse with no budget for any of those advertised materials. And due to my health, I also didn't have the physical energy to be creating DIYs and setting up activity after activity. I started to wonder, back then, if maybe I wasn't giving her "enough," and my heart broke. I knew, logically at least, that this wasn't the truth and that the joy and well-being Montessori brings has so little to do with the "things." Yet, if I could be influenced by the social media world, even as a certified Montessori educator, I wondered if others were aching from this, too. It was then that I focused on realigning my mindset, and soon opened up my very first Montessori Peaceful Parenting course. To my surprise, it sold out right away—as did the next, and the next, and the next! Over the years, I've had the honor of working with and guiding tens of thousands of parents all around the world with a heartfelt invitation to embark on a conscious, compassionate, and joyful parenting journey.

It has been the adventure of a lifetime and I now live with absolute certainty that I am and always have been exactly where I'm meant to be—even if it was a bumpy road that led me here. So, I thank you with my whole heart for giving me the space and opportunity to be your peaceful Montessori parenting guide.

Kindly, Haley

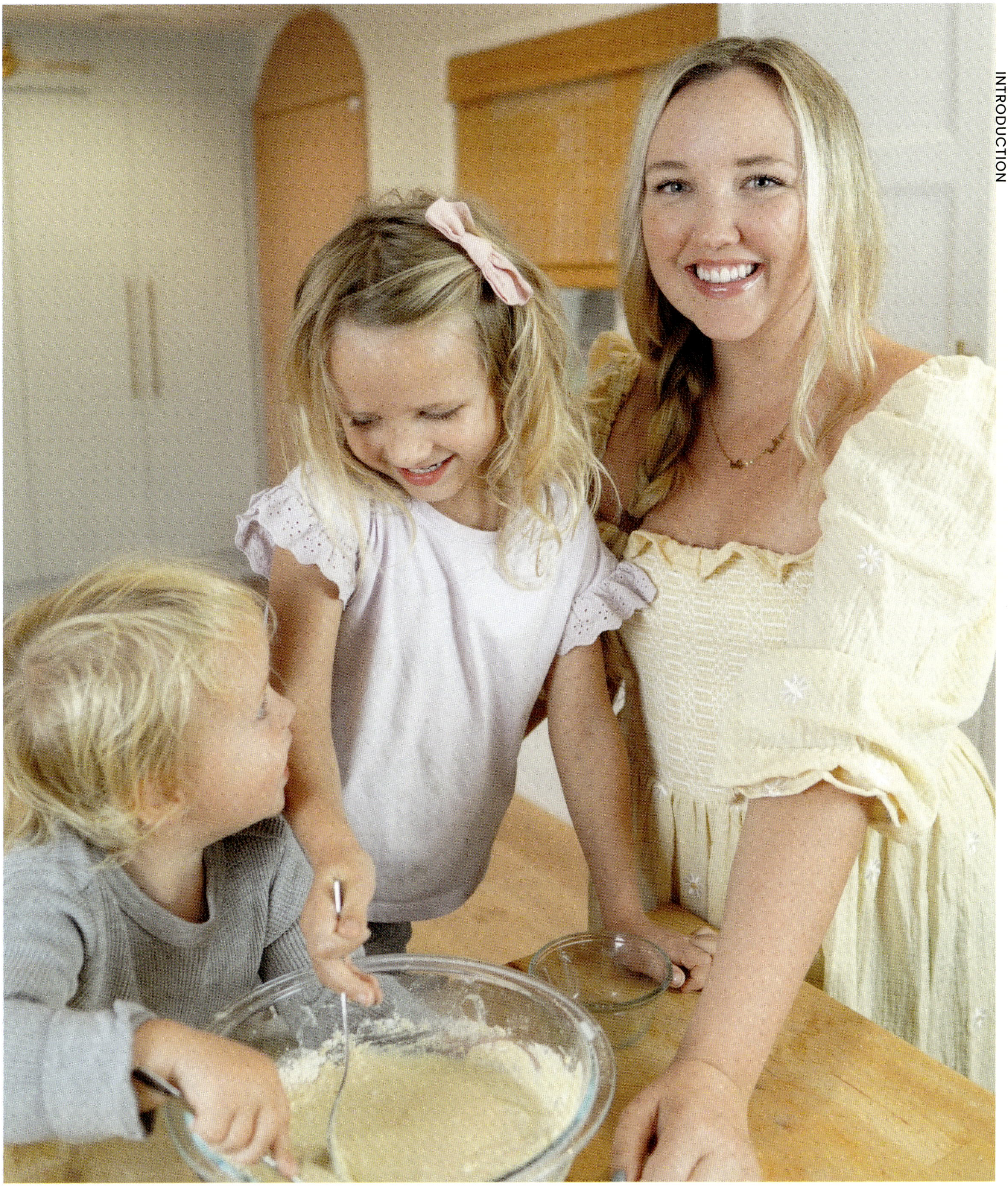

Foundation

By breaking down the essentials and celebrating those who dedicated their lives to this incredible work, we find new ways to appreciate and apply these methods every day. This chapter is a heartfelt tribute to Montessori's legacy, others who support our journey, and a friendly guide to bringing their wisdom into our lives. We'll soon build on these timeless principles and all the magic they bring into our homes, helping us practice peaceful parenting and create nurturing spaces for our little ones.

THE HEART OF MONTESSORI

Before we bring this into our family lifestyle, let's do some background housekeeping and explore the heart of Dr. Maria Montessori's philosophy and approach to teaching and learning. The Montessori Method was developed by Dr. Maria Montessori, an Italian physician and educator, in the early 20th century. At its core, Montessori emphasizes the following principles:

- **Child-Centered Learning:** The method is built around the belief that children are naturally curious and eager to learn. It recognizes that each child is an individual with their own unique interests, abilities, and learning pace. Guides in Montessori classrooms strive to meet each child where they are in their development and provide an environment that supports their natural inclination to explore and learn.

- **Prepared Environment:** The method is carefully designed to create a stimulating and child-friendly environment that's filled with hands-on materials and activities that allow children to independently explore and engage in self-directed learning. The materials are designed to be self-correcting, enabling children to learn from their own mistakes. The Montessori school environment is based on the home, as home is where little ones feel most safe, secure, and able to flourish.

- **Freedom and Responsibility:** The method encourages freedom, within limits. Children have the freedom to choose their activities, work at their own pace, and explore their interests. With this freedom comes the responsibility to make choices, complete tasks, and respect the needs and work of others in the classroom.

- **Mixed-Age Grouping:** Montessori classrooms have mixed-age groupings, allowing children of different ages to interact and learn together. This arrangement promotes social development, peer learning, and collaboration. Older children can serve as role models, and younger children benefit from observing and working alongside them. This transfers organically to supporting siblinghood and the varying ages/stages throughout the family.

- **Teacher as Guide:** Montessori teachers, often referred to as guides or facilitators, play a supportive role. Rather than standing in front of a full class of children and dictating, their role is to observe each child's progress and provide guidance and materials based on individual needs. The teacher's role is to foster independence, encourage exploration, and offer assistance when needed or requested.

- **Self-Directed Learning:** The method emphasizes intrinsic motivation and self-directed learning. Children are encouraged to follow their interests, ask questions, and explore subjects in-depth. This approach helps children develop a love of learning, true understanding of self, and the ability to think critically.

- **Holistic Education:** The focus is on the development of the whole child, encompassing not only academic, but also social, emotional, and physical growth. Activities in the Montessori classroom often integrate various subjects, senses, and aspects of development.

- **Peace and Respect:** Values are promoted such as respect for others, empathy, conflict resolution, and a sense of responsibility for the environment. Peace education is a fundamental aspect of Montessori philosophy, fostering a sense of community and social harmony.

These principles are at the heart of Montessori education and are designed to help children become independent, lifelong learners who are well prepared for academic success and positive, peaceful contributions to society. Montessori is often applied in early childhood education, though it continues on into elementary, middle, and even high school levels.

BEYOND THE SHELF

Bringing Montessori into your home, beyond the shelf, refers to the concept of applying these principles and philosophies past the traditional materials or curriculum. We're looking deeper into our parenting experiences to simplify and hold onto the foundation of what makes such an impact—even, and maybe, especially with less of the "stuff."

Children don't need to go to a Montessori school or homeschool or have any of the materials in order to benefit from the adults in their lives seeing them with deep respect and kindness.

What we call *peaceful parenting* in today's world is a dive into the way Montessori educators are trained in being with children. It can feel complicated on so many levels, but at the end of the day, the parent–child relationship is just that—a relationship. A relationship that requires nurturance, understanding, unconditional love, and strong roots. We ultimately seek to peacefully coexist with these small children in a way that honors who they are, as well as who we are.

By looking beyond the beautiful shelves and aesthetic of Montessori, we unearth a hidden path of age-old wisdom. This path isn't lacking in potholes, forks-in-the-road, or steep drops off cliffs, to be honest, though it's also abundantly full of wildflowers (for those who make time to see them), a reliable GPS, safety barriers, and helpful speed bumps.

It's Dr. Montessori's work paired with the modern-day researchers, advocates, and educators that offer clarity and guidance. Montessori beyond the shelf is accessible to everyone and is truly where the long-term well-being of our kids is founded.

I have every ounce of respect and admiration for the didactic Montessori materials and those incredible classroom experiences. To walk into a true, qualified Montessori classroom is to be mystified by the way these guides support their class. The joyful little workers, peaceful buzz, and flowing community are like nothing I've seen before. The experience is profound. Research even stands aligned with higher adulthood well-being for those who attended Montessori schools in childhood.

That said, one of the latest studies currently circling the media has revealed in its conclusions that there may be a factor we haven't considered, or for the sake of the research, haven't yet been able to study. And that is, in the words of Lillard, Meyer, Vasc, and Fukuda (2021), "Although this study only shows an association between Montessori schooling in childhood and higher adult wellbeing, lottery control studies and studies showing that features of Montessori schooling are associated with higher wellbeing in other settings lend weight to the possibility that Montessori might cause higher adult wellbeing. But if this isn't the case—if in fact features of Montessori parents or some other third variable associated with Montessori attendance is the cause—then it would be very interesting to determine what the underlying cause for the discovered association is."

Wouldn't it be worth wondering what the role of those "Montessori parents" has on this study and its impact on the child's wellbeing—not only this study, but in real life, spanning across the globe?

The amazing thing is, as you read further in this book, you'll see just how aligned Montessori parenting is with the newest science on raising kids with intention, consciousness, and connection.

A BRIEF HISTORY

Maria Montessori was an Italian physician, educator, and innovator in the field of education. Her life and pedagogical philosophy are deeply intertwined. Here's a brief overview below of her history and the development of her work.

Early Life and Education

Maria Montessori was born on August 31, 1870, in Chiaravalle, Italy. She initially pursued engineering, entering an all-boys technical school at the age of thirteen. She later decided to study medicine, becoming one of the first women to attend medical school in Italy. Let us just take a moment to honor what that would have meant for her and the women who followed in breaking that glass ceiling. Incredible, isn't it?

How the Montessori Method Came to Be

Maria initially concentrated on psychiatric medicine in her early career. However, her interests gradually shifted toward education, prompting her to enroll in pedagogy courses and dive deeply into educational theory. Her academic pursuits led her to critically evaluate the conventional methods employed in teaching children with intellectual and developmental disabilities.

In 1900, her opportunity to enhance these techniques arose when she accepted the role of codirector at a new institute aimed at training special education teachers. It didn't take long for the program to be celebrated as a success, as many of the children displayed unexpected progress. With her unique roots firmly in science, Maria meticulously observed and experimented in her teaching methods. The innovative methods at this institute laid the foundation for her pedagogical principles.

In 1907, more clarity on her methods came to be when she agreed to establish a full-day childcare center in San Lorenzo. This center catered to underserved and unsupervised children from ages three to seven in the impoverished inner-city district. This became the very first *Case dei Bambini.*

Applying scientific observation and drawing from her prior work with young children, Maria developed educational materials and classroom settings that nurtured children's innate desire to learn and granted them the freedom to select their materials. She observed how these young learners effortlessly absorbed knowledge from their surroundings, effectively teaching themselves.

To the astonishment of many, children enrolled in Maria's programs thrived, displaying heightened concentration, attention, and spontaneous self-discipline.

The Worldwide Spread

In 1909, Maria Montessori published her book, *Il Metodo della Pedagogia Scientifica applicato all'educazione infantile nelle Case dei Bambini,* which was later translated into English as *The Montessori Method.* The book outlined her pedagogical principles and gained international attention.

The success of the Case dei Bambini and her work led to the rapid spread of Montessori education worldwide. By the early 20th century, Montessori schools were established in countries across Europe and the United States. Maria Montessori's work earned her international recognition and numerous awards. She also conducted training courses for teachers interested in implementing her method. And while she led this movement, she also urged people to understand that she wasn't seeking to be a "pioneer," saying that the children showed her the way and wanted the main focus to remain on the children, not adult ego. Dr. Montessori hoped the children could be seen as the leader in this, in their homes and schools, through all their developmental needs.

Further Developments

Over time, Montessori continued to refine and expand her educational approach. She developed materials and techniques for various age groups, including preschool, elementary, and even secondary education. Her work incorporated elements of child psychology, child development, and pedagogy.

While Maria Montessori's work was primarily focused on education, her impact on gender equality and empowerment can be seen as a form of early feminism. She played a significant role in challenging gender biases and advocating for the rights and potential of girls and women, both in education and in society at large.

Having lived through such turbulent times, she strongly advocated for peace in leadership. Through these experiences, she developed Peace Education as a foundation in her method. It was her belief, and ours still today, that by raising generations of children who embrace living respectful, peaceful lives, they will contribute to future world peace.

The Years to Come

During World War II, Montessori was exiled from Italy for her refusal to support fascism. She continued her work in India, training teachers and refining her methods even further.

Even though Maria could have returned to Italy at the war's end, she chose to spend her final days living in Amsterdam. She passed away peacefully in a dear friend's garden on May 6, 1952, at the age of eighty-one.

Legacy

Maria Montessori's educational philosophy, often referred to as the Montessori Method, has continued to influence early childhood education and beyond. Her emphasis on child-centered, hands-on learning, mixed-age classrooms, and respect for the individual child's natural development remains central to Montessori education.

Today, Montessori schools and Montessori-inspired educational practices are found around the world, and her ideas have left a lasting impact on how we approach education and child development.

PEACEFUL PARENTING

In this book, we'll refer to the aligned parenting methods under a blanket term of *peaceful parenting*. In truth, though, what we know about child development and parenting spans over many decades of research: centuries, even. Along with Dr. Montessori, there are quite a few major contributors in the fields of child development, psychology, and education who laid the groundwork for our present-day understanding in raising the next generation, rooted in peace, connection, and unconditional love.

Peace is a core principle in the Montessori Method and is integrated into every aspect of her work. This foundational hope of real and true human peace is weaved into the preparation of self as the guide, the fostering of peaceful conflict resolution in the children, the intentional and respectful treatment of every single material, plant, pet, or human friend, and in the knowledge that at their core, children are these profoundly good beings. And truly, no matter the outward behavior we see, they're good, good, good; they might just need a little help navigating the world and their emotions.

We, today in 2024, are just coming around to seeing this truth. Yet, when she spoke it, it was new. Or maybe, rather, it was lost, long before. This idea that a child is inherently pure and whole from the start, and to be cherished as such, was a direct contrast to what many believed of children in generations before us. Children were often seen as an empty vessel, waiting to be manipulated and shaped to their adults' liking.

What I find as the greatest honor to teach a generation of parents isn't my own work. It's the work of the many before us, lighting the way, paving the road, dedicating their lives, and tirelessly advocating. These brilliant names are worth knowing and thanking for their contributions to what we have accessible in knowledge today.

Let's start a little ways back. Not all the way back, but at least to who was making these leaps forward in the 20th century. Let's meet some of the major influences:

18

- *Alfred Adler,* an Austrian medical doctor and psychotherapist, contributed significantly to parenting with his belief that human behavior stems from a desire for significance and belonging. Despite their different paths, both Montessori and Adler have similar views on the importance of nurturing and respecting the individuality of each child; their work often compliments each other's.

- *Jane Nelson* developed the Positive Discipline Program based on Adler's principles, fostering responsibility and respect in the parent–child relationship. Montessori schools around the world have adopted this method of discipline.

- *Magda Gerber's* RIE approach advocates for sensitive caregiving and respecting infants' autonomy.

- *John Bowlby and Mary Ainsworth's* attachment research underscores the importance of secure emotional connections in child development.

- *Erik Erikson's* psychosocial theory informs parenting approaches that nurture emotional growth. He was Montessori-trained and certified, which invites us to consider what influence her work had on Erikson's developmental model.

- *Diana Baumrind's* work on parenting styles promotes empathy and setting boundaries.

- *Dr. Haim Ginott's* work as a renowned clinical psychologist and psychotherapist helps parents gain more empathy and calm in raising kids.

- *Adele Faber and Elaine Mazlish* offer practical guidance for peaceful parenting through communication techniques.

Contemporary authors like *Daniel Siegel, Tina Payne Bryson, and Shefali Tsabary* contribute to peaceful and conscious parenting practices, emphasizing modern brain science, mindfulness, and emotional attunement.

The list could truly go on and on!

Peaceful Montessori parenting is really a multifaceted approach that emphasizes the importance of self-awareness, emotional attunement, empathy, and mindful presence in parent–child interactions. It's important to note that modern peaceful parenting techniques draw from a combination of these theorists and others, and they continue to evolve with ongoing research and insights in the fields of psychology and child development. Montessori's philosophy, aligning with research of her own and that of theorists past and present, advocates that effective discipline should be kind yet firm, respectful, and designed to encourage children to realize their own capabilities.

While it's this foundation of research that we've built upon, what many discover is that once you hear it, learn it, and begin to truly understand it, you will likely find that it feels natural and instinctual. And as you flow from day to day, loving, keeping safe, and growing alongside your child, it may begin to feel like this is how it was always "meant to be."

This is what we mean by the wisdom of Montessori. It's not just a scientific method of education, it's a guide to feeling whole and held as a mother, a father, a grandparent, a teacher, and as a friend. Because when *you* feel held and supported, the children in your life get the opportunity to feel the same.

THE MONTESSORI TRIAD

At the heart of Montessori education lies a powerful concept known as the Montessori Triad—a harmonious relationship amongst the child, the environment, and the guide. This triad forms the foundation of Montessori philosophy and plays a pivotal role in creating an experience that nurtures the child's holistic development.

To honor the importance of the Montessori Triad, the first three parts of this book are an expansion of exactly this!

19

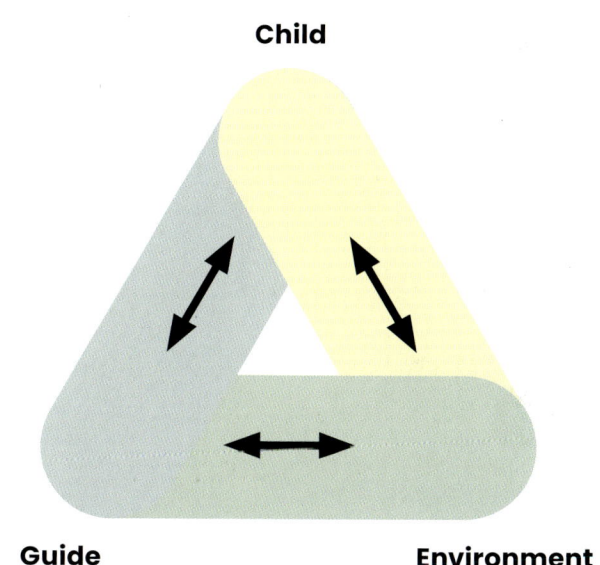

Child

Guide　　　　　　　　**Environment**

1

The Guide

In the Montessori Triad, the guide plays a vital role as a facilitator of learning rather than a traditional teacher. The guide observes the child's interests, provides support, and creates an atmosphere of respect, trust, and cooperation. They act as a bridge between the child and the environment, helping the child navigate their education and journey of self. *You,* dear magical parent, are the guide!

PREPARATION OF THE SPIRIT

By releasing the traditional ideas of filling children with information, as if they're an empty vessel, we let go of the abundant stress of such a role. When we instead see the child as a full, capable, and independent being, we understand that the whole philosophy is really about cultivating a lifestyle that allows the child freedom to safely explore and grow into their truest potential. We have the crucial role of creating a space of calm and nurturance, rather than chaos or hindrance. A parent's role is the biggest influence on the child's long-term health, emotionally, cognitively, and physically.

The key pillar here is the inner work—which, as we all know, can be the hardest work. When we're open and honest about our own intentions, values, and biases, we're then able to show up for our children in the ways they need. Dr. Montessori called this the "preparation of the spirit." Learning how to fully respect children takes a high level of peace and understanding in ourselves, before we can extend that to our kids.

It's helpful to make a shift into seeing our family as our closest community, and for a community to thrive, we must meet the needs of all. A conscious approach to raising children will never mean putting the adults' needs aside; in fact, as parents it's crucial that we put our own oxygen mask on first. And while we all know how difficult that concept is to fathom, it's deeply worth repeating and breaking down, so that all parents and caregivers grow into seeing their own needs as truly valuable and worth honoring.

Only when we meet our own needs can we meet the needs of our children and see our little family community flourish. In short, for them to grow and bloom, we should grow and bloom alongside them.

"As parents become more aware and emotionally healthy, their children reap the rewards and move toward health as well. That means that integrating and cultivating your own brain is one of the most loving and generous gifts you can give your children."

—DR. DANIEL J. SIEGEL

RESPECT & WHY KIDS DESERVE IT

I've asked the same question to thousands of parents in workshops and almost every single person has nearly the exact same answer.

The question is, "Why does your child deserve respect from you?"

Please write your answer down here:

_____

_____

_____

In traditional parenting paradigms, it's often believed that respect is earned; that a child isn't deserving of respect unless they've shown that they're worthy of it. A parent, though, is to be respected in every single moment, interaction, and situation. So they say, anyway.

Many, maybe most, of us were raised in a paradigm like that—one where the adult demands respect, yet may often be disrespectful and possibly even hurtful to the child. It doesn't appear or feel to be a loving and connected relationship, and many raised in such a way are ready to break that cycle in their own parenting.

Now, when I ask that question of respect to parents all around the world, the answer, with some variation, is almost always this:

"They're human."

Simple. It's so simple.

As Dr. Maria Montessori said, "Children are human beings to whom respect is due, superior to us by reason of their innocence and of the greater possibilities of their future."

Children are these profoundly pure, beautiful humans with a whole and expansive life ahead of them—their potential is boundless. A child comes into this world needing and expecting to be loved and cared for. The treatment they receive from us becomes the treatment they feel they're worthy of. And for the sake of humanity itself, they are, by design, as "respectful" as they're able to be at any given time. They're so reliant on their adults, actually, that they will do anything for the love, connection, and safety that they need. When love, connection, and safety are inconsistent or absent, that's often when we see those cries for help that appear to be "attention-seeking behavioral issues." But more on all that soon.

They're the future. They're world changers. Our giving them their rightful place as worthy humans doesn't need to exempt us adults from the same. Yet, their innocence, their reliance on us to protect and love them, should hold some sway in the goodness and understanding we treat them with, too.

The child, as they grow and receive "respect," can grow to give respect, built upon the grounds of a loving relationship and bond. As we adjust our expectations to understanding development, some basic neuroscience, and emotional intelligence, it becomes clear why children struggle to show an adult "respect," as defined by the traditional way of raising kids. That traditional definition, if we're being honest, is really *obedience*. Blind obedience, at that. While blind obedience is convenient—a "yes, ma'am" instead of a tantrum does sound easy, I'll agree—there are actually some serious potential consequences of this goal.

Consider this question: "Is obedience synonymous with respect?"

We may be obedient to a cruel boss who controls our income, health care, and work life. Yet is that actually respect that we feel toward them? Can you think of anyone who regularly punishes or shames you whom you deeply respect? It's unlikely. Respect has so much more depth—so much more beauty. To gain the respect of our children is an incredible thing, a thing of great influence. Influence, actually, that's more "effective" long term than just about anything else.

So, is it mutual respect we want reciprocated through our modeling? Or is it blind obedience we aim to demand?

As peaceful parents, we honor and respect our own children by treating them as individuals with their own thoughts, feelings, and rights, while also guiding and supporting them in their development. It is a normal and healthy part of development for children to ask questions, push back, and even refuse an adult's demands; it is also essential for reasons of safety and consent that a child knows they can protest and say "no," even to an adult.

INTENTIONS, VALUES & ACTIONS

Intentions

Without setting clear intentions of what we're doing *and* where we're planning to go, we can end up just about anywhere, lost. By bringing intention to our existence, though, we have a say in where we end up. It's in the clarity that we stop drifting about, unsure of how to get to wherever we're going. When we set clear intentions, it's a beacon of light guiding us through the night, through the storms, and even reflecting the sun on those beautiful days. Always there, never too far away, and the constant we all need as humans.

Values

Values play a crucial role in shaping your intentions and actions as a person and parent. In establishing what our values are, we're clarifying our priorities. For example, if you hold empathy close to your heart, you might find yourself focusing more on nurturing a strong emotional bond with your child rather than strictly "teaching lessons" in certain moments. This understanding of what truly matters to you helps in setting meaningful goals, too. Say, if you value family togetherness, your plans might include organizing family activities or enjoying meals together.

When it comes to making decisions, your values act as a compass. (So you've got an intentions lighthouse and a values compass now; seriously, you'll never feel stranded in Parentville again.)

For example, if you establish honesty as a cornerstone, you'll naturally gravitate toward open and honest communication with your child, especially during those tough talks. This approach not only helps in the moment but also brings consistency to your parenting style. Aligning your actions with your values in this way creates a stable and predictable environment for your child, which is essential for their sense of security.

Parenting isn't without its challenges, and here, too, your values can offer much-needed guidance. If patience is a virtue you uphold, you'll find yourself working hard to support difficult behaviors with a calm and understanding demeanor.

It's also vital to regularly reflect on your parenting practices, ensuring they align with your values through different ages and stages. This self-assessment is crucial for maintaining authenticity in your role as a parent. By consciously identifying and regularly revisiting what matters most to you, you can foster a purposeful and intentional approach to parenting, one that resonates deeply with both you and your child.

Actions

Every day, we have a million chances to integrate and be guided by such intentions, informed by your values, and to take action.

As we all know, we can sometimes *act* in a way that's deeply misaligned with our intentions and values. It's those actions that wreck a parent with guilt or shame. "Mom guilt" and "Dad guilt," are such buzzwords these days, yet often miss the context for parents on how to feel less of those feelings. When we come to understand what it is that lights that little flame of shame, it's all much easier to navigate.

The more often we act out of alignment with our intentions and values, though, the wilder that shame flame grows. And the more shame we feel, the worse we feel about ourselves as parents, the more we come to believe it defines our parenthood, and the less able we feel to make changes. A tricky cycle.

You see, a universal truth about humans, young or old, is that when we feel bad inside, we're more likely to act "bad" outside. In other words, if the cycle a parent is trying to break is to stop yelling, they could have set that intention and it would probably be informed by a core value of connection and patience. They strive to respond to their child in attunement and understanding; yet, in the moment, their actions were misaligned, and they yelled. Yelling was misaligned with the parent or person they're trying to be, and *if* that shame flame lights and grows wilder, possibly by feeding it with thoughts like, "I'm such a bad parent," "What's wrong with me?" "I can't do anything right"—then that's the view of self they'll settle into. It'll continue to be the story they tell themselves, and if they don't find clarity in how to act in alignment with their intentions and values, then the more likely they'll be to continue yelling, then feeling shame, disliking who they're showing up as, and then acting out of alignment again. As you see, shame, whether it's placed onto us by ourselves or by someone else, doesn't help anything. You're a good person doing the best you can at any given time with the tools and skills you have available to you, and the same is true about your child. The difference is, we have a whole lot more ability to learn new tools and skills with our fully developed brains and nervous systems.

It helps tremendously when you're confident that your growth and "cycle breaking" are being led by your values. So, let's really dig deep and I'll invite you to read through some of the values listed to the right. As you look at them, notice how each word makes you feel. Does it speak to you? Does it feel like a guide to you? Please write down your top ten of them—or create your own list if you do not see the values that are held nearest to your heart.

Respect
Integrity
Empathy
Peacefulness
Faith/Faithfulness
Compassion
Responsibility
Honesty
Authenticity
Gratitude
Generosity
Perseverance
Patience
Kindness
Tolerance
Forgiveness
Cooperation
Teamwork
Loyalty
Open-mindedness
Humility
Accountability
Optimism
Courage
Self-discipline
Self-respect
Equality
Connection

Simplicity
Mindfulness
Love
Justice
Fairness
Caring
Appreciation
Tolerance
Flexibility
Resilience
Innovation
Curiosity
Creativity
Independence
Health
Adventure
Environmental stewardship
Spirituality
Balance
Authenticity
Harmony
Wisdom
Learning
Adventure
Resourcefulness
Simplicity
Freedom
Trust

Core Values

And then, narrow those ten down to three. Those three can be considered your *core values*. These are the core values that guide you, inform your intentions, and carry you in parenting, or life in general, when things get hard. Lean into, fall into, ram into, full-speed crash into them, and they'll remain true to you. We all deserve to know and feel held by our own values. It makes acting in alignment with them a whole lot easier when we set conscious intentions to honor them.

One of the most effective ways to implement your core values in daily life as a family is to create a list of family guidelines in your home. We do this by sitting down together, kids included, talking about what values matter most to each of you, and making a list of rules or guides that every person will do their best to follow based on those. It also gives everyone in the family a sense of ownership around these family guidelines, and are thus more likely to follow them. When someone acts outside of the guidelines, we support them in getting back into alignment with those values, reminding them of the rules you created together. Not in a lecture-y way, but just as a reminder that you're all in this together—a team, looking to help each other thrive.

OUR FAMILY GUIDELINES

We will always try our best to be kind

We do not hurt each other

We do not hurt ourselves

We take care of our environment

We take care of our bodies

All feelings are welcome

Use the QR code to print out your own Family Guidelines, or see page 215.

THE TEN PILLARS OF PEACEFUL MONTESSORI PARENTS

There are ten pillars of peaceful Montessori parenting that I want to share with you. Ten ideas, mindset shifts, guides and thoughts that will help to inform your every decision in raising children. They're informed by core values, yet also by modern-day child development and neuroscience. The overall theme of each pillar is to choose love and empathy—to choose connection and to choose the parent–child relationship.

The purpose of creating this list is to offer one more resource for those moments where raising children begs the question, "What am I supposed to do now?" Whether it's a challenging behavior to respond to, a decision to be made, an interaction to be had—it helps beyond measure to have pillars like these as your foundation.

1. **We're not here to control our children—our job is to control ourselves.**

   Releasing the idea that children need to be "controlled" is one that takes a lot of unlearning. It's not our job to control anyone, other than ourselves. We can control our response to the behavior of others—whether that be a choice to respond calmly, react in rage, find kindness and empathy, or blow up is up to us. In the case of parent–child relationships, our job is always to control our own behavior above all else. This doesn't mean that we forgo holding clear, consistent, and firm boundaries where needed. Boundaries aren't the same as control. Control's aim is self-serving and holds risks to the impact of a child's true self, their confidence, their willingness to "cooperate"/collaborate, and more. Not to mention, we really can't control anyone, not even our own child. We all realize that when faced with a child who doesn't eat, sleep, or pee on our demand. They're human, not robots, after all.

2. **Children learn more from the behavior we model than what we try to "teach" through words.**

   Children aren't influenced by the words of hypocrites, and while that may sound harsh, it's deeply true. If we hope to raise kind humans, we must be kind humans. If we hope to raise kids who don't yell, hit, shout, and coerce to get their way, we must not do such things to them or others. Raising children invites us to do the work to become a version of ourselves that's *better*. Full of goodness, kindness, and self-confidence. Children absorb who we are, not what we say.

> "The question isn't so much 'Are you parenting the right way?' as it's: 'Are you the adult that you want your child to grow up to be?'"
>
> —BRENÉ BROWN

3. **It's not our child's job to make us happy—our happiness is our own job.**

The manipulation done to children in the name of making them responsible for our feelings is more devastating than one might realize. Pleas drenched in blame like, "You're making mommy sad by being a bad listener." Or "Daddy will be so upset if you don't take a few more bites of food." Or "Why do you have to make mommy so mad? I wouldn't have to yell at you if you didn't make me so angry" are an unfair "tool." They play to the desperation of children who are likely to override their own will and sense of self to please their parents. A child shouldn't bear the weight of "making us" feel anything. And while we do want our kids to understand that their actions affect others, we don't want to make them feel *responsible* for others' feelings. Beliefs like, "I'm too much," "I'm in charge of my parents' emotions," or "I'm to blame for daddy's angry outbursts" can stem from this. By adjusting our language and owning our own emotions, we spare them this. Doing that could sound like validating and even at times voicing our emotions: "Love, I'm feeling really frustrated right now and I need a moment to cool down." This is an example of ownership of our own feelings and modeling regulation tools, without shaming or blaming anyone else.

4. **A child presenting challenging behavior is a child who needs our help.**

This shift has preserved my relationship with my children, time and time again. Emotional development, age, impulse control, and many more factors go into why a child presents "challenging behaviors." There's always a need beneath the behavior, or a skill still being developed, and once it's met, the challenging behavior ceases to exist. When the child screams and cries in a tantrum, they're screaming and crying for help. That help might be a need to co-regulate, a sensory need, a need for clearer and more consistent boundaries, a need for independence or to feel more significant in the home—detecting what that need is, is our job. And when we consistently choose to help, and not hurt, they can trust us that we're on their side.

5. **The depth of our connection is the only true influence we have in their choices as they grow.**

Research shows that the more connected a child feels to their parents, the more influence they have on their behavior. While coercive parenting tools like yelling, bribes, and punishment may "work" when the child is young, as they grow and are out of the home more often, it's that parent–child bond and internal moral compass that acts as a guide in their decisions and behavior.

6. **Come from a place of compassionate curiosity when responding to their behavior and your own.**

Invite yourself to become a compassionate and curious parent. The act of putting your hand on your heart, saying, "Wow, this looks very hard for them; I wonder what's going on" and responding in that way feels better for *us* and the child. Likewise, if we react to our children in ways that are out of alignment with our values, rather than placing shame into ourselves, we can offer that same compassionate and curious embrace. "Hmm, this is really hard for me. I wonder what this is revealing to me? Is this an unhealed wound? Is this a coping mechanism retained from childhood? Or maybe I just forgot to eat breakfast and I'm hangry?" Get curious. You are *good*. You're a person worthy of compassion. You are loved and deserve to understand more about what, inside, makes it difficult to respond in connection with others, and maybe even with yourself.

7. **Treat the child with the utmost respect for the person they are and the person they're becoming.**

Montessori really believed in giving kids the highest level of respect and treating them with genuine kindness. By seeing them as their own people with endless possibilities, we hold space for them to grow into who they're meant to be.

8. **Our role isn't to mold them to our liking, it's to support them as they discover who they are.**

We're the guides of our child's upbringing, through guiding alongside them. We're not to manipulate, mold, shape, or chip them away into our ideal design. It's possible to guide by tending to, nurturing, creating the proper environment to thrive, and honoring their uniqueness.

9. **Attention-seeking behavior is connection-seeking behavior.**

Somewhere along the way, attention became known as an undesirable behavior, rather than an innate human need. A child and an adult both need attention—there's nothing wrong with the child hoping to gain ours. And while the word *attention* can be off-putting, their real goal is connection. When they actually receive that connection and the feelings of significance and belonging that they (and all humans) require to thrive, the child can rest and feel less burdened by the need to gain "attention."

10. **We're our child's world. They don't want to make us angry or upset. They're always doing their best.**

"They're just doing it to make me angry," or "They only do this behavior because they know it'll get under my skin." These are things we hear often, said about children by their parents. Yet, we're their source of life, safety, wellness, food, security. They *need* us. They don't want to make us angry or displeased; just simply by human design, that idea threatens their survival. They may, however, feel desperate at times and seek that connection through means of any attention possible. There comes a time where any attention, even yelling or anger, is better than no response at all. There's an African proverb that holds the weight of this truth. "The child who isn't held by the village will burn it down to feel its warmth." How profoundly sad is that?

Children are doing the best they can in any given moment based on the tools they have and the age/stage of development they're in. Growth isn't linear, and when we see them as just people learning how to be a person for the very first time, we see the truth of the beautiful little being in front of us.

THE PARENTING PARADIGMS

Parenting paradigms refer to overarching frameworks or models that influence how individuals approach and understand the task of parenting. These paradigms encompass a set of beliefs, values, attitudes, and practices that guide parents in raising and nurturing their children. Different parenting paradigms reflect diverse cultural, psychological, and social perspectives.

While the terms *parenting style* and *parenting paradigm* are related and share some similarities, they aren't identical and are used in slightly different contexts.

Parenting style refers to the typical manner in which parents interact with their children and the overall emotional climate they create within the family. A parenting style primarily focuses on the behaviors and attitudes that parents consistently exhibit in their interactions with their children. This is often categorized based on two dimensions: responsiveness (or warmth) and demandingness.

Research on parenting styles, particularly the four classic parenting styles proposed by Diana Baumrind, outlined below, has been extensive and spans several decades. Diana Baumrind's initial work on parenting styles was incredibly influential, and researchers have since built upon and refined these concepts. Research has explored the impact of parenting styles on various aspects of child development, including academic achievement, social competence, emotional well-being, and physical and mental health. *Authoritative parenting* is consistently associated with positive child outcomes, while the others are less consistent and do yield higher rates of undesirable and unfortunate outcomes for children.

Parenting paradigms, however, refer to a broader, overarching framework or model that considers cultural, psychological, and social influences. They focus on the overall approach or philosophy that parents adopt in their parenting journey, considering not only specific behaviors but also the underlying beliefs and values shaping those behaviors. This, as you've likely come to realize, is why I've asked you to really explore and ground yourself in your own personal values.

In essence, while parenting styles are a component of parenting paradigms, the latter includes a wider array of influences on parenting practices.

Authoritative
Create positive relationship, enforce rules

DEMANDING

Authoritarian
Focus on obedience, punishment over discipline

WARM & ACCEPTING

COLD & UNACCEPTING

UNDEMANDING

Permissive
Don't enforce rules, "kids will be kids"

Neglectful/Uninvolved
Provide little guidance, nurturing, or attention

Unpacking Command/Demand Parenting

In the world of parenting, the *authoritarian style* stands out for its emphasis on control and strict rules, creating a dynamic that's often compared to a dictatorship, with the parent in charge and the child at the bottom of the hierarchy. This approach is characterized by a clear "my way or the highway" attitude. Phrases like, "Do what I say right now and no back talk," are common in such households. It's a world where rewards and punishments hinge on the child's obedience, often tying their sense of worth to how well they fit into this rigid structure.

The core belief of authoritarian parenting is that the parent knows best, holding all the authority, knowledge, and decision-making power. This top-down approach leaves little room for kids to have a say, expecting them to follow rules without question. The focus is on the adult's authority, often overlooking what the child might need or feel, or where they are in their growth and development. It's like the parent is holding a sign saying, "I'm in total control here."

Tools like time-outs, grounding, or the silent treatment are go-to strategies in this style, with rewards being the flip side of the same coin, still used to control behavior.

At the heart of this is "adultism," a way of thinking that puts adults above children just because of their age. It's like saying adults are always smarter and more capable—and kids? Well, they just don't know enough yet to have real autonomy or deserve the same level of respect.

Growing up in such a paradigm can be tough on a kid's view of self, as well as the bond they have with their parents. It's a setup where kids are pushed to meet adult standards, often ignoring their unique needs or developmental stage. This imbalance can stifle open communication, limit a child's growth in independence, and lead to a strained relationship. While some studies show that kids from authoritarian homes might be good with self-control, discipline, and schoolwork, we have to ask, "At what cost?" These possible benefits are often overshadowed by drawbacks like low self-esteem, social struggles, and a higher chance of feeling anxious or depressed. The strict rules and lack of emotional warmth can make it hard for kids to solve problems or be independent. Plus, these kids might end up either rebelling or being overly submissive, finding it hard to stand up for themselves or make their own choices.

For parents who now find themselves in this type of paradigm and want to show up differently for their own children, know that at any time you can choose a different story for your family—a path that's not just about being fair and just, but also about being nurturing and supportive, helping yourself and your children grow in a healthy way.

Permissive Parenting

In permissive parenting, parents tend to adopt an overly relaxed approach, often characterized by leniency and a high degree of freedom for their children. These parents are usually very loving and nurturing, but they might struggle with establishing firm boundaries or enforcing consistent discipline. It's important to recognize that having flexible boundaries in certain areas doesn't necessarily mean a parent is permissive; there's a broad spectrum in parenting styles.

It's also worth clarifying that permissive parenting is distinct from concepts like "gentle" or "conscious" parenting. They're often confused by mainstream media, but they're not definitely synonymous.

Permissive parents are typically very responsive to their children's emotional needs, often prioritizing the child's immediate happiness over a need for boundaries. This can lead to a household with little structure or routine, where children may not have clear expectations set for them. In such environments, decision-making can be heavily influenced by the children, potentially overshadowing the much-needed guidance of their parents, which can be very unsettling for a child. And while it may appear that a child wants this "control," it's not developmentally appropriate and actually leads them to feel out of control. A child needs to be able to safely rely on their adult as a confident and kind leader.

The reasons behind a parent's permissiveness are often more complex than a simple reluctance to enforce rules. It could stem from a feeling of inadequacy in fulfilling the parental role or from a deeper, perhaps unconscious, belief system where the child is viewed as holding more authority. This isn't about parental laziness or indifference; it's about challenges in coping with the demands of parenting, like communicating effectively or setting empathetic limits.

Interestingly, individuals who grew up in highly authoritarian homes may sometimes adopt a permissive parenting style as a counter-response to their upbringing. Their past experiences, where self-assertion or boundary setting were met with negative consequences from adults in their lives, can really influence their approach to parenting today.

However, it's important to understand the potential implications of permissive parenting. Children raised in such environments might struggle with understanding and respecting boundaries due to the lack of consistent rules. This can manifest in challenges with impulse control and decision-making. Additionally, the absence of clear guidelines can hinder the development of self-regulation and emotional management skills in children. They may also find it difficult to take responsibility for their actions—a crucial skill in social interactions and relationships.

Neglectful Parenting

Neglectful parenting, now recognized as one of the main parenting styles, was a later addition to Diana Baumrind's original classification. Unlike permissive parenting, which may lack structure but offers warmth, neglectful or uninvolved parenting is characterized by an absence of both emotional involvement and boundaries. This style often stems from complex circumstances, where parents may struggle with mental health issues, substance abuse, overwhelming stressors, or simply lack the necessary parenting skills. As a result, they may find it challenging to provide the care and attention their children need, leading to significant emotional and developmental consequences for the child.

Understanding neglectful parenting involves acknowledging that these parents might be grappling with personal struggles, such as limited emotional or financial resources, that leave them overwhelmed and unable to adequately meet their child's needs. It's a situation where empathy for the parent's situation coexists with the acknowledgment that such an upbringing is unjust and harmful for the child. In some cases, neglectful parenting behaviors are unintentionally replicated from the parents' own experiences of neglect or emotional distance, perpetuated by a lack of positive role models or guidance.

Research consistently shows that children from neglectful homes often struggle with emotional regulation, forming secure attachments, and cognitive and academic development. They may exhibit behavioral difficulties like aggression or withdrawal and face long-term challenges in forming healthy relationships, maintaining self-esteem, and are at a higher risk of mental health issues. Neglectful parenting is also linked to increased substance abuse and delinquency in adolescents.

Support and education can open doors to interventions and support systems for struggling parents, fostering healthier environments for both parents and children—because every child deserves unconditional love and a nurturing environment to grow and thrive.

Discovering the Peaceful Parenting Paradigm

Understanding our why, and truly believing that who we are *makes sense,* is a beautiful gift to behold. It helps to bring awareness to our experiences, reassure ourselves that *if* we've been parenting outside of our actual values, in misaligned paradigms, there's nothing wrong with us. It's crucial to acknowledge that your parenting style is a reflection of your unique life experiences. Change is always possible, and growth is a continuous process. Embracing this understanding can be empowering, allowing you to make conscious choices to show up as the parent you hope to be.

We explored the depth of a paradigm briefly, and what really makes a paradigm more significant than a parenting style is the values and beliefs that inform them. It's not enough to teach a new skill set, offer "tips," or even share the research. A true change comes from understanding the mindset, the experiences, the deep-rooted conceptions of power, authority, and how they play into the way we parent.

In our modern world, with information at our fingertips, we can be informed in every parenting choice we make, if we choose to be. That research, consistently and overwhelmingly, supports an *authoritative parenting style;* we consider this the style that informs the Peaceful Parenting Paradigm.

Authoritative parenting, marked by a warm and responsive approach coupled with clear expectations, fosters a nurturing environment where children can thrive. With open communication, mutual respect, and a balance between warmth and structure, authoritative parents provide guidance while encouraging independence. This parenting style is associated with positive outcomes such as higher self-esteem, better academic performance, strong social skills, and overall well-being. The emphasis on understanding a child's perspective and involving them in decision-making cultivates a sense of security and confidence. These parents are adept at setting boundaries with empathy, allowing for a supportive and loving atmosphere that promotes the whole child. A whole child approach is about helping kids grow in every way, not just academically, but emotionally, socially, and physically too.

I wonder if we may be able to reconnect to some of our parenting intuition and inform that intuition with this amazing research to begin trusting ourselves in the ways we show up for our children (and ourselves). What I mean by this is: I truly believe that in your heart, in your soul, you have a guide full of wisdom on how to nurture your child.

We do, however, also have the history of humanity impacting how well we can feel that inner guide of ours. It's not untrue that humans would have inherited effects on our nervous systems of wars, genocide, colonization, industrialization, and our own family generational traumas. Who you are, your nervous system, your *being,* in many ways, was inherited. You aren't defined by these things, but they're part of your story. Every human has a different story, and wherever you are on your journey of healing and peaceful parenting won't be the same as your neighbor. Not because Sally down the street is *better* than you. Not because Monique is a perfect parent and you're broken—you're always *whole,* always. But this is what being human is. Inherited truths, influences, experiences, support, lack of support, and circumstances that were out of your own control—yet more reasons to give yourself grace and consider an empathetic view of your own experiences today.

"When a flower
doesn't bloom, you
fix the environment
in which it grows,
not the flower."

—ALEXANDER DEN HEIJER

As we explore your values, intentions, and beliefs, you'll personally uncover and code your own way of peacefully existing with and relating to your child. This is very much where Dr. Maria Montessori's work comes into play. The work she guided her teachers in wasn't just academic. It was the depth of respect she had for every single child, and the passion in which she revealed the sacred truth of children to the teachers she trained. To see the child not as an empty vessel in need of coercion to perform, but as a free spirit worthy of respect, beyond the goal of simply getting kids to "obey."

The quote below is one of her many clever ways of describing and inviting us to honor the unique child in front of us, without threats, bribes, or punishments. Her work, the lifetime of research in observation and being with children, offered us so much. And do consider being a woman in this field one-hundred years ago, when a man's word was so dominant, that she shared such profoundly contrasting insight on child rearing and education. At this time, the world was very fixated on a behaviorist way of controlling children—in many ways, that's still true today.

While she loved those free-spirited children, many thought they would run wild and chaotic without such methods of control. Yet, in her schools, they were so beautifully peaceful. You see, respecting the true nature of children doesn't mean chaos. It means, rather than seeing the child as a problem that needs our fixing, we see them as whole, and create a peaceful, secure environment that allows them to flourish in every way.

We focus on connection and a healthy attachment in the parent–child relationship, where there's a balance of warm nurturance *with* clear structure and consistent boundaries, which children require to feel safe and calm.

"Rewards and punishments are . . . the worst enemies of the natural development of the child. The jockey gives sugar to his horse before the race, but applies spurs and the whip when there is lagging. Still, do any of these methods induce the animal to run as swiftly and as superbly as the horse of the plains?"

— MARIA MONTESSORI

A Montessori approach embraces the idea that though it's our role to care for the child, we're no more significant than they are. There's true equity in the relationship. While the child's brain is still in development and they're in fact in *need* of us—our attunement, our safety—that doesn't mean we're above them in any made-up hierarchy. A child's significance in this world and in our families is deeply important. While you are a provider of food, shelter, love, and consistency, the child is a provider of joy, wonder, connection, will, and the true goodness of humanity. They don't owe us that. They don't *have to* provide such gifts, and yet, they do—simply by their nature of being. When we step back and look at how much they give, while different from our purpose as adults, the child's purpose is magnificent. There's no need to tally up how or why a child deserves to be seen as an equal, as we aren't trying to pit ourselves up against them in any way, but if we were going to play such a game of tallies, wouldn't we agree that their value is truly significant in this world? That they're worthy of equity? That they teach us the meaning of life, every single day, in the awe of which they view the world and the genuine kindness that they show every living being they come across?

In this book, we explore what it means to have equity in a parent–child relationship, understanding that it's not about being equal in roles—parents and children naturally have different ones. Equity is about fairness and justice, ensuring each child gets what they need to thrive, whether that's resources, guidance, or attention, tailored to their unique stage of life, personality, and personal experiences. Because, truly, being "fair" doesn't mean everything is exactly the same, not even for each sibling. What it means is that everyone's needs are met, so they can thrive.

If you're older than around the age of twenty-six, you happen to have a fully formed prefrontal cortex, and for that reason, have a way easier time managing your emotions. Yes, it takes that long to develop! You, being the older person, have a lot to offer in this parent–child relationship and in a peaceful parenting paradigm—we value understanding that. We also value understanding where our children are developmentally, all the many ways they're unfolding in the human process. We're then able to align our expectations in ways that allow us to exist *with* our children and grow *with* them.

Research has also uncovered significant associations between parenting styles across generations; "bad" parenting appears to be passed down as much as "good" parenting. This means for those of you here reflecting on how you were raised, we're all more likely to simply pass this on than to change. Generation after generation of repeated cycles is no coincidence. Those raised in stressful environments often become accustomed to a fight-or-flight response, leading their nervous systems to unconsciously seek out similar situations as adults. This familiarity with stress can result in a preference for known, albeit negative, circumstances over unknown, potentially positive ones, as the nervous system favors familiar patterns. That means a child who's raised in a household where shame, blame, and punishment are typical, will likely go on to think that it's in fact normal—not only normal, but acceptable, and what they're worthy of.

Our goal is to treat our children with so much respect, kindness, and love, setting healthy boundaries and creating a peaceful atmosphere, that with the first signs of anything other than that goodness, they know it's not acceptable. We set the stage for our children's future relationships, making us the architects of their understanding of love and connection. Let's draw every road on their map with love and intention, guiding them toward a future filled with respect and empathy.

The Weather

It's us that creates the weather. The parent, teacher, or caregiver turns a tornado into a peaceful day or a gust of wind into a hurricane. This is a beautiful and powerful gift, to be used for good, light, and positivity. This power of yours, this weathermaker that you are, comes from neuroscience and attachment science—deep in our human-ness, we're influenced by our parents, for many, many reasons. One reason is that children need you for survival. Simple. Another is they need your love. Pure. Another is something called *mirror neurons*. Requiring no conscious intention of our own, mirror neurons, in the most basic terms, create messages to those around us for when it's safe to feel calm, peaceful, and when it's time to freak the heck out.

But how? How do we manage our own emotions? Own our hurricanes? Well, it takes work! Let's begin by acknowledging that we're all only human. Practicing peaceful Montessori parenting doesn't mean we can, need to, or should be only calm all the time, every single second of the day. What a bland human existence. You're meant to feel the range of human emotions. You're meant to feel them with passion and courage. You're also able to do that in a safe way—safe for you and safe for your child.

"I've come to a frightening conclusion that I'm the decisive element in the classroom (home). It's my personal approach that creates the climate. It's my daily mood that makes the weather. As a teacher (parent), I possess a tremendous power to make a child's life miserable or joyous. I can be a tool of torture or an instrument of inspiration. I can humiliate or heal. In all situations, it's my response that decides whether a crisis will be escalated or de-escalated and a child humanized or dehumanized."

—HAIM GINOTT

SELF-CARE

Taking care of *you* is so often overlooked in parenting, yet it's what replenishes your emotional and physical reserves, helping you better support yourself, and therefore, your children. More often than we realize, those moments of parental rage don't stem from the child "being difficult"; they stem from deep exhaustion, lack of support, and depleted self-nurturance. They have more to do with us than them. Remember, you can't pour from an empty cup, and true self-care is more than how the media portrays it. We want to focus on activities that restore, rejuvenate, and nourish the mind, body, and soul. That sounds more ethereal and intangible than it is, so let's explore!

A vital aspect of self-care is setting boundaries to protect your personal time and needs, learning to say no when necessary. Nurturing relationships with your partner, friends, or support networks through meaningful conversations and activities can also bring immense joy and connection. Incorporate mindfulness practices like meditation or deep breathing exercises to center yourself and reduce stress.

As we briefly explored a few sections back, a parent's own life experiences and biases significantly impact their parenting styles and behaviors. Understanding these aspects of ourselves allow us to recognize how past experiences might influence our reactions, beliefs, and perceptions of the children's behaviors. Aligning with this is the high value of healing practices like therapy, because the most profound and beautiful gift we could ever offer our children is our own healing.

Engage in physical activities that you enjoy, like yoga, walking, or dancing, to feel energized and uplifted. Spending time outdoors, journaling your thoughts, feelings, and gratitudes, or engaging in hobbies and self-expression, such as painting, writing, or playing music, are all ways to nourish your soul. Prioritizing adequate rest and quality sleep plays a crucial role in mental and emotional well-being, too. The irony isn't lost on me that I'm telling a bunch of parents of young children to prioritize rest. I assume you're doing the best you can there. No one needs one more person to say "sleep when the baby sleeps"—but how about a reminder instead that your value isn't tied to your productivity, and that it's not only okay but valuable to plop onto the couch and *rest* instead of running around "getting things done" into all hours of the night.

Eating healthful, balanced meals is another form of self-care. Don't just settle for eating scraps off your kids' plates in a rush; take time to sit down and enjoy your meal. You deserve to nourish your body—it's so important to hold boundaries around this! That might sound like, "Oh yes, love, you want me to play with you right now. I see you've finished your lunch and I'm still eating. You go ahead and play; I'll let you know when I'm done."

Parenting partners may consider making consistent self-care plans to keep on the calendar, whether they're daily, weekly, or biweekly. Remember, as parents, we're models for our children. Do we want to raise kids who link their value to busyness, even if that means neglecting their own needs? Or do we want them to see us taking care of ourselves, setting healthy boundaries, and pursuing our passions and interests? Our self-care isn't just for us (though *you* deserve it!); it's also for your children, influencing them to live a balanced, peaceful, and fulfilled life.

"The real preparation for education is the study of one's self. The training of the teacher who is to help life is something far more than the learning of ideas. It includes the training of character; it is a preparation of the spirit."

—MARIA MONTESSORI

THE ATTUNED PARENT

To be attuned in parenting means being deeply connected and, you guessed it, *in tune* with your child's emotions, needs, and experiences. Attuned parenting involves actively listening and observing, seeking to understand your child's perspectives and feelings without judgment or imposition. It's about being present and *responsive,* adapting your parenting approach to meet your unique child where they are emotionally and developmentally. This concept in parenting emphasizes empathy, validation of emotions, and nurturing a strong and secure attachment with your child.

Attunement isn't always instinctive and no one can be perfectly attuned at all times—and that's okay. No one can be perfect, in any way, all the time. And perfection absolutely isn't the goal—we'd all go mad if that was the case! We just want to show up as our authentic selves, genuinely putting in effort to grow, and stepping up with our best foot forward as often as we're capable of. It's quite the practice in mindset shifts. A practice that involves being aware of our own emotions, too. In a world where we're often taught to suppress feelings, learning to truly "feel with" rather than just "deal with" emotions is crucial for being responsive and attuned to our children.

For those raised in environments where emotions were dismissed or punished, like being sent to time-out for crying or being urged to suppress negative emotions, attuning to a child's emotions can be challenging. Our own emotional upbringing plays a significant role in how we're able to connect with our children.

So, where do you start? It's simple, really. Just listen. The first step in attunement is actively listening. Simple yet profound, active listening—giving full attention, echoing their words, and showing understanding—makes children feel heard and significant. This fosters an environment of validation and understanding, strengthening the parent–child bond and building trust. It's not just about hearing their words; it's about tuning into their emotional world, even if they're nonverbal. Observing cues and emotions helps us connect with their experience and understand the child on a much deeper level.

By setting an intention to fully listen to our children and to truly see them beyond the behavior and into the reasons beneath them, we gain insight into their thoughts, feelings, and perceptions, allowing us to respond more effectively to their unique needs. This deep understanding and connection are at the heart of peaceful and conscious parenting.

An attuned parent is also one who can *follow the child.* In Montessori, this is all about tuning into each child's unique rhythm, interests, and developmental needs. Think of it as a gentle guiding process rather than a strict teaching method. It's like walking alongside a child on their learning journey, rather than leading them down a predetermined path. This nurturing approach not only encourages kids to explore and learn at their own pace but also reinforces their self-esteem and independence. When we follow the child, we're showing them that they're valued and understood, laying the groundwork for a strong, loving relationship. It's a wonderful way to ensure that learning and growing up are filled with joy, respect, and mutual trust. It also saves us the stress of getting our child to fit into a specific box. We see them for them, and choose to follow their needs, interests, and calls for either independence or support.

"Anyone who wants to follow my method must understand that he should not honor me but follow the child as his leader."

—MARIA MONTESSORI

TRIGGERS

Triggers are emotional responses or reactions that stem from past experiences, often linked to unresolved or unhealed wounds, traumas, or stressors. In parenting, triggers can significantly impact a parent's ability to be conscious and present. They can throw us out of attunement, to put it lightly. When triggered, emotions overshadow rational and compassionate responses, leading to reactive or automatic behaviors that may not align with parenting goals.

These triggers may arise from various sources, such as one's own childhood experiences, cultural influences, societal pressures, or personal insecurities. For instance, a parent who experienced criticism or neglect in childhood might react strongly to perceived rejection from their own child. Similarly, cultural beliefs or societal expectations about parenting might trigger feelings of inadequacy or self-doubt.

"Triggered" is quite the buzzword, and understanding your own triggers is indeed vital to a more conscious approach to being with children, yet every reaction that you have is not to be blamed on a trigger. Triggers are specific and do have an anchor to earlier (not exclusive to childhood, but often from childhood) specific experiences or traumas. You may notice a trigger by a conscious observation that your own reaction could be considered as very intense, or maybe blown out of proportion, for that moment or challenge.

Here is a chart that outlines common parenting triggers alongside possible reasons based on the parent's own childhood experiences.

Without conscious intention and awareness of a trigger, the brain forms an association/connection between the trigger and your response to it, so that every time that thing comes up again, you have the same behavioral response to it. This is because "what fires together, wires together," as Dr. Dan Seigel explains. That means, when neurons fire in the brain, they wire together the situation, emotions, and responses that caused that firing of the neurons in the first place.

So, rather than strengthening those triggering connections, we want those neurons firing in a positive way—toward healing. This takes intention, repetition, and hard work.

Once we begin to recognize when they happen, we can see triggers for what they are—overreactions to a perceived threat. Then, we can learn to respond in ways that are more life affirming, useful, and healthy for us and our children. This involves a process of self-awareness, self-compassion, and intentional healing.

"Between stimulus and response there is a space. In that space is our power to choose our response. In our response lies our growth and our freedom."

—VIKTOR E. FRANKL

Here are some of the basic steps making new neural connection toward healing:

- Notice the message your body is trying to send you
- Notice the emotions that are pulling you toward an automatic reaction
- Resist your automatic reaction
- Redirect your impulse to a healthier one

By actively working on healing triggers, parents can cultivate emotional resilience, which enables them to respond consciously and compassionately to their children.

As triggers are stimuli or events that elicit intense emotional or psychological reactions in individuals, often linked to past traumatic experiences or unresolved issues, then we consider *glimmers* as the exact counterpart. These are moments or instances of positivity, hope, or strength within one's mental health journey. Glimmers can be seen as small sparks of resilience, moments of joy, progress, or coping amidst challenging or difficult circumstances. They provide a sense of encouragement and motivation, indicating progress or the potential for improvement.

Common Parenting Triggers	VS	Possible Reasons for the Trigger
Child expressing big emotions		Past experience of being shamed, ignored, or punished when expressing big emotions
Child being loud, silly, or rowdy		Childhood experiences of being told they're too much, annoying, or bothering others
Child not listening to rules or following directions		Experiencing inappropriately high expectations in childhood
Child asking questions or disagreeing		Past experiences of command/demand parenting & not being allowed to voice opinion
Children having a conflict or sibling rivalry		Unresolved sibling conflict or competing for parental attention
Child either being reserved or extroverted in social settings		Past experiences of shame for the way they existed in social situations (i.e., "too shy" or "too loud")

APOLOGIES, FORGIVENESS & TRUST

The trio of apology, do-over, and forgiveness forms the bedrock of nurturing and healthy parent–child relationships. They not only strengthen the bond between parents and kids but also create a supportive environment that's essential for growth, emotional well-being, and mutual respect. Every relationship to come into your child's life will have ruptures—friendships, siblings, school/work companions, romantic relationships—all of them have potential for challenges. *While ruptures, fights, mishaps, challenges, tiffs, all can happen—it's how we repair that matters.*

Apologizing plays a critical role in peaceful parenting. When parents acknowledge their mistakes and say sorry, it's not just about admitting "errors"—it's about showing humility and being accountable. This builds trust and respect, teaching kids that everyone makes mistakes and it's important to take responsibility for our actions. An apology also gives us a powerful model in healthy conflict resolution and emotional regulation. Here is a helpful step-by-step.

After an apology, asking for a "do-over" or a "re-do" is invaluable. This strengthens neural connections, helping both you and your child understand how a situation could have been handled differently. It's a form of practice for your brain to respond better in the future and shows your child the kind of behavior they should expect—respectful, loving, and firm when needed. With time and practice, your automatic responses will become more confident and connective.

And while verbal apologies are great, remember that every interaction with your child should feel genuine. There are many ways to connect and repair, and a step-by-step verbal apology like this is just one of them. For any script in this book, or elsewhere, know that it's just an outline and meant to offer insight and ideas. Your words should feel genuine and authentic to you, not like some robot parent reading a teleprompter. Your kids love the real you.

When kids see their parents apologizing, it also nurtures their ability to forgive, key to healthy healing and learning from mistakes. Forgiveness lets both parents and kids move forward, viewing mistakes as learning opportunities rather than as sources of conflict or emotional distance. Remember, it's crucial to respect a child's process in forgiving, and equally important to forgive ourselves to move forward with growth in mind.

Two key ideas here:

- The child can take as long as they need to process their forgiveness. Since the goal of forgiveness is to reestablish trust, it's important that they see us respecting their process. Step back and hold space for this.

- Forgiving ourselves is vital to moving forward with the goal of growth.

Repairing ruptures leads to trust, which is the foundation of any healthy relationship, and this is especially true in the parent–child dynamic. It reassures kids that their parents are committed to growth and improvement. Keep in mind that yes, we're human, and though we won't show up perfectly in every moment, we do want to be working on the thing we're apologizing for. Saying "sorry" only to go right back into a yelling fit feels very disingenuous and confusing for a child to process. "I'm sorry" should mean something to us and to our children.

Apologizing to Children

Recognize that you acted outside of your values.

Acknowledge that your actions do not fit within the intentions you've set as a parent. Your core values as a parent should act as a guide in letting you know when an apology is due. Approach the apology without shame or blame.

Take responsibility and be specific.

To help a young child conceptualize, tell them the story of what happened. Be specific in taking responsibility: "You had milk in your cup, and then you poured it on the rug. Oh no! A big mess! And then mommy yelled. I was very upset and I scared you, right? No more yelling, mama!"

Reconcile. Apologize from the heart.

Offer a big hug. "I love you and I am sorry I yelled." Give yourself a do-over if appropriate. "It is never okay for me to yell at you like that. Let me try that again. I should have said . . ."

Resolve by focusing on a solution.

Brainstorm an agreement that will be respectful to fix the problem or prevent it in the future.

THE TRUTH ABOUT DISCIPLINE

When you think of "discipline," does "punishment" come to mind? That's a common reaction, but actually, discipline is all about learning and teaching, stemming from the Latin word *disciplina*. Think of your child as a little disciple who's better off learning the value of good behavior rather than just fearing negative consequences. Dr. Dan Siegel puts it so well: "Effective discipline isn't just about stopping bad behavior or encouraging good ones, but about teaching skills and nurturing connections in our children's brains for better future decisions and behavior."

Discipline is incredibly important for young children. And contrary to what some might think about peaceful parenting, it's not about being permissive; it's about striking a balance with what I call the 4 Cs: being connected, calm, consistent, and clear. Our role is to teach socially acceptable behavior, to guide them in "freedom within limits," as Maria Montessori said. This means granting them freedom, holding space for them with love, while also setting limits so that they don't have to feel chaotic, lost, and unruly. Because while it may appear that the child wants all control, that isn't the case. In fact, that lack of parental guidance and boundaries is very scary for them! What they need is to feel safe and secure while exploring the world around them. So we show them that we're the peaceful and confident guide on which they can depend. Above all, we don't allow them to hurt themselves or others, or mistreat materials or

their environment. The weight of those behaviors, and feeling out of control in their own bodies, can negatively impact their view of self. Remember, while we often follow the child's lead, we're still the guide in this relationship.

Help is knowing *how* to decode the behaviors and the needs, even for the child who's asking for that help in the most difficult ways.

The traditional view of discipline is that our children "behave" because they learn to be scared of us. This creates not only disruption in the parent–child relationship, but emotional pain, as well. You see, punishment robs children of their own critical thinking—they comply with our demands out of fear instead of understanding the reasons why positive

behavior is important. They instead "behave well" because they've been coerced into that. One of the major problems with using punishment as discipline is that children learn extrinsic/external motivation (to behave through fear of being punished) instead of intrinsic/internal motivation (to "behave" because they are internally motivated to behave).

Peaceful Montessori parenting isn't an assortment of quick tricks. What we're doing is building a respectful relationship with our children. There should be no act of discipline that doesn't first serve to connect with the child. Our connection is grounding. Our connection is what helps teach them. Our connection is essential.

"To let the child do as he likes when he has not yet developed any powers of control is to betray the idea of freedom."

—MARIA MONTESSORI

UNCOVERING NEEDS

To uncover the need beneath the behavior of young children means embracing a compassionate approach that goes beyond surface actions. It involves recognizing that every behavior is a form of *communication,* a way for a child to express their needs, feelings, or desires. Instead of focusing solely on the outward actions, we strive to understand the underlying emotions and motivations. We see only the tip of the iceberg, the behavior itself, while 90% of the iceberg remains unseen underwater.

Behind every behavior, there's an emotion, and behind that emotion is a need. When we take care of that need instead of just dealing with the behavior, we're getting to the heart of the matter, the root cause—not just slapping a Band-Aid on it.

Below is a simple chart illustrating examples of typical early childhood behaviors and potential underlying needs that could be uncovered:

> "Either we spend time meeting children's emotional needs by filling their cup with love, or we spend time dealing with their behaviors caused by their unmet needs. Either way we spend time."
>
> —PAM LEO

ILLUSION OF MISBEHAVIOR

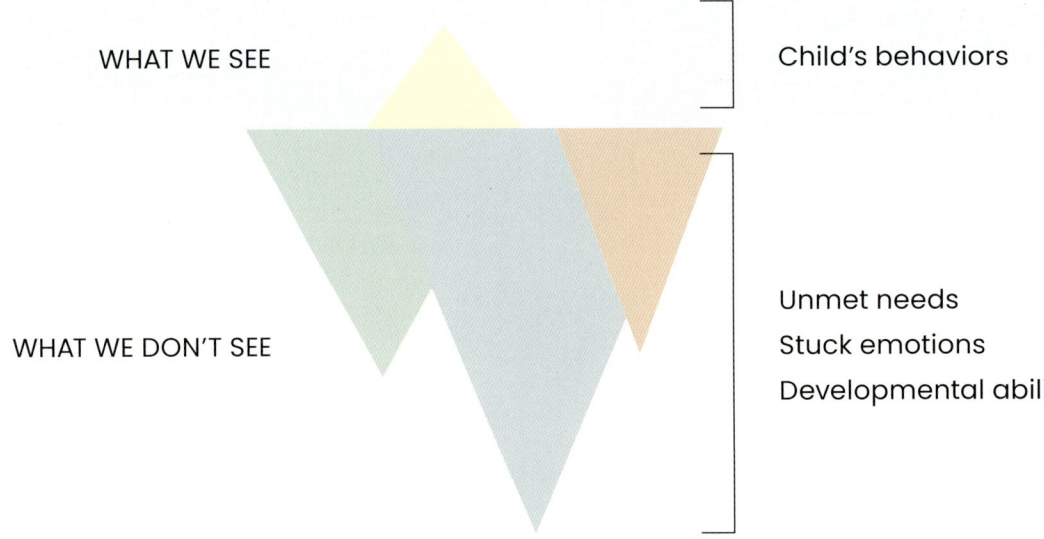

WHAT WE SEE — Child's behaviors

WHAT WE DON'T SEE — Unmet needs / Stuck emotions / Developmental abilities

Behavior	Potential Underlying Need
Tantrums or Meltdowns	Lack of autonomy and choices, feelings of frustration, fatigue, sensory overload
Withdrawal	Anxiety, need for comfort and security
Aggression/Defiance	Frustration, lack of autonomy, connection seeking
Clinging/Neediness	Insecurity, need for reassurance, connection seeking
Resistance to Transitions	Fear of the unknown, need for routine
Excessive Energy/Restlessness	Lack of physical activity, boredom, sensory needs
Crying/Whining	Physical discomfort, emotional distress, connection seeking
Refusal to Eat/Sleep	Control, discomfort, anxiety, sensory needs

This chart is just a starting point, and each child is unique, but it's helpful to bring this type of compassionate curiosity to difficult moments.

EMPATHETIC LIMITS

Empathetic limit-setting in parenting is like setting up guardrails with heart. Instead of just laying down the law and dishing out punishments, this approach is more about guiding the child.

Let's break it down: It starts with talking to kids in a way that truly respects their emotions and gives them a voice. This not only strengthens communication but also builds a solid foundation for your relationship. Consistent, empathetic boundaries are key here. They help kids learn to manage their own behavior in a positive and supportive environment, rather than feeling scolded or misunderstood.

Trust plays a huge role in this approach. Kids are more likely to respond positively and accept guidance when they feel heard and understood. This builds a sense of security in their relationship with you as their caregiver.

Empathetic limits also encourage a sense of independence, where kids have opportunities to make their own choices and learn from their experiences, all within a supportive and safe environment—without the fear of harsh consequences.

In practice, setting empathetic limits is a balancing act of clear expectations and allowing children the freedom to express themselves and learn. A key aspect is using "and" instead of "but" when setting limits. For instance, saying, "I understand you want to play longer *and* it's time for bed," connects two truths. It shows empathy and also affirms your role in setting necessary boundaries.

Another crucial element is "connection before correction." Before correcting a behavior, it's important to connect with the child emotionally, acknowledging and validating their feelings. This approach ensures that children are more receptive to guidance because they feel cared for and understood. It's also a reminder not to yell something from across the room and expect a child to "listen." Children are often so submersed in their own world that they're unable to process what it is we're saying from afar without the point of connection first.

Of course, there are exceptional situations involving immediate danger where swift action is needed. But generally, these moments are rare, and the focus should be on empathetic, understanding, and nurturing limit-setting.

parent's intentionally set guardrails

child's safe and prepared path

Here is a simple guide to setting empathetic limits, using hitting as an example:

1. Set the boundary

"I won't let you hit me—hitting hurts. I need to keep my body safe." Block the hitting or step aside, if you must.

2. Validate the feeling

"You really want to hit right now. I know it's hard. It looks like you feel angry. It's okay to feel angry. And I can't let you hit."

3. Promote the *yes*

"You can touch me gently."
"You can give your body a squeeze-hug."
"You can stomp the angry feelings out on the rug."

4. Model the appropriate emotional outlet

In this case, model healthy aggression outlets like stomping, yelling into a pillow, dancing, Tarzan yelling outside, etc., and invite the child to join. Aggression isn't an inherently bad thin—it just requires a safe release. Be sure these skills are being taught outside of the moment of difficulty so the child has practice and is more likely to be able to access the tools during hard moments.

5. Supervise

Stay close by. Stay as calm as you can. "Catch the behavior" before it happens again. To stop these behaviors, the neural connection must be stopped/broken by preventing or interrupting the behavior. For example, if we walk away and the child hits again, they've completed the neural connection, strengthening that response circuit. By being present and stopping the behavior from happening again, while modeling a different tool, the circuit was broken, rather than strengthened. We focus on strengthening the positive tool instead.

Another helpful tip is to keep the 4 Cs in mind while setting a boundary. Here are some examples:

Calm

Take a deep breath and regulate your own nervous system, first.

Connected

Make a connection with the child. This may be as simple as a gentle hand on their back, a look of empathy, or an acknowledgment of their feelings/interest in that moment. "Oh wow, you're so interested in throwing right now. I see that."

Clear

Be intentional about words used, telling the child what's okay rather than only focusing on what not to do. "That's a hard ball. We can only throw soft ones in the house. I'll help you find one."

Consistent

If you've set a boundary, be sure to keep it consistent. For example, the next time the child throws a hard ball in the house, even if it's a week later, maintain the boundary and follow through.

Examples of calm, connected, clear, and consistent interactions:

- "I know you're having so much fun playing. It's hard to stop! *And* now it's time for dinner."

- "I understand why you would rather stay at the playground. Yes, we can definitely come back tomorrow *and* now we need to go home. I'll help you to the car."

- "You're showing me you don't want to brush your teeth right now *and* so let's make it more fun! I can race you there! Let's go!"

- "You don't want to go to bed. I hear you, bub. *And* it's bedtime. Is it your turn to pick out a story or mine?"

- "I know you want to keep painting all night! I get it. You love art! *And* it's still time to clean up. Your artwork will be waiting for you in the morning. Would you like to leave your supplies here to pick up where you left off tomorrow? Or we can put them away together. You decide."

And of course, follow through with whichever they decide. If no decision is made, the parent will make the decision. When we consistently set limits and follow through, the child learns that our words are worth something. One thing to consider, is that *you're* the one setting and holding a boundary. Boundaries aren't about *telling* the child what they can't do and expecting them to follow through with it on their own; rather, we're *showing* the child what we won't allow and following through. What does that look like?

Telling a child:

"Don't throw that toy! I've told you so many times. Don't throw it!"

Telling a child something is a lot like making a request. We expect them to follow through with it themselves, even though this is often not a developmentally appropriate expectation.

Showing/holding a boundary:

"I can't let you throw the toy. I'll help and put it away for you until another time."

The boundary doesn't request anything from the child. We see that the child is doing something unsafe, and so we tell the child what we're going to do to stop the behavior and follow through.

We mean what we say, and that's incredibly valuable to consistency in the relationship and in a peaceful home overall. It's their right to dislike a boundary or protest against it *and* our role is to hold it. Remember, all feelings are welcome and all behaviors are not.

Holding boundaries with empathy and a goal to actually discipline by *teaching* has such profound long-term impacts. Because no matter how many rewards we give, or punishments we threaten, we can't control what our children do when there's no one around to enforce them. But we can nurture their critical-thinking skills, moral compass, compassion for others, internal drive, and self-control. And therein lies your greatest influence on your child's long-term success and well-being. There's immeasurable difference between coercing a child into behaving compared to establishing an environment where they actually want to and have the tools to regulate themselves and make good choices.

THE EXPECTATION GAP

A child's self-esteem is closely tied to how well they believe they're meeting the expectations of others, especially their parents. When parents set appropriate expectations, children feel successful and valued, and a child who feels good about themselves is more likely to exhibit more positive behaviors. If expectations are unrealistic, however, a child's self-esteem and self-worth can take a hit.

It's surprising to note that a recent study revealed 56% of parents think children under three can resist forbidden impulses, and 36% believe children under two can. But research indicates that impulse control starts developing around three-and-a-half to four years of age. Similarly, 43% of parents expect children under two to share and take turns, a skill that typically emerges closer to four years old. (See Resources, page 216, for more information.)

This is called the *expectation gap*. Much of what parents consider "bad behavior" is actually developmentally appropriate behavior—it is the expectations that need adjusting. So often kids are punished for things entirely outside of their control or abilities. *Understanding and setting realistic expectations for children's behavior and development is crucial.* It accounts for a significant part of parenting, actually. And while something may be developmentally expected, it doesn't mean we just let it happen. For example, it's developmentally normal for a toddler to hit, but we don't just let it happen and we're going to talk about that soon.

There's the reverse side of the expectation gap, too. Children hold expectations in their own minds about the way any given moment will pan out. They have expectations on the way we (and all others) will respond to them, the way a theory of theirs will unfold, the way something will feel, look, taste, etc. The trouble is, parents often overlook the expectations that a child has and how to support them when things do *not* go as they expected, planned, or theorized. Bridging that gap for a child brings a sense of overall ease to their lives, an ease that supports their development of self.

"You didn't expect that to happen, did you, love? Yeah, that's very hard," is one of my most used statements in raising and working with children.

Sometimes that moment arises when our child runs into the room excited for morning cuddles only to see that the baby is already there, nursing. Maybe this is a moment out of the typical routine, when she usually wakes up before the baby and gets some quality time with parents. Her *expectations* of the morning didn't pan out, which brings up a lot of big feelings.

Maybe it happens when they've built a giant tower and go to put that final piece on, thinking it's about to complete their brilliant masterpiece, and then the entire thing falls down on them.

It could be when they see their older sibling doing a puzzle and expect that it'll be okay with sibling to join in, and then it turns out sibling actually needs some alone/down time to work by themselves.

Our kids are making tens of millions of new neural connections every day. In the first few years of life, more than one million new neural connections form every second. They're making theories and hypotheses, testing cause and effect, and creating expectations about all of these things. The emotional load of it all can be so overwhelming for them, especially when they feel they keep miscalculating. So one of the best things we can do is set their little world up for consistency and bridge those expectation gaps with them.

MELTDOWNS, TANTRUMS, CO-REGULATION

Imagine difficult feelings as tunnels. We're just chugging through them like trains, heading toward that peaceful light at the end. You know, we have to ride through all the darkness to get there. Have you ever tried rushing out of an emotion tunnel before you're really done feeling the feeling? The darkness doesn't disappear—rather, it just hides deeper inside of us. For a healthy mind and nervous system, we want to feel it through, fully.

When our little ones are tangled up in emotions like sadness, anger, fear, or embarrassment, our go-to move is often trying to talk them out of it with logic. We explain why they're overreacting, or how *we* know it'll turn out just fine in the end.

We're trying to help our children, of course, but if we peel back the layers a bit, let's be real: Deep down, we're kinda trying to soothe our own discomfort because our kids feeling pain hits us hard. Of course it does. We love them so deeply.

It's also very possible that if emotions weren't welcome in your childhood, the sight of them in your child now may be triggering. Or maybe emotions like anger or sadness were too big or too scary from your parents, and made you feel unsafe. It makes sense that now your first instinct says to shut it down in the child. This is why it's so important to reflect and be aware of what beliefs and ideas come with us into parenting.

But here's the deal: Our job isn't to raise a human who only feels safe or acceptable when they feel/appear *happy*. We don't need to snap our fingers and make our little ones joyful ASAP. This is where we see parents distracting kids from feeling the feeling or "giving in" on a boundary to stop the crying. Our role, though, is to be the supportive guide—the helper, not the fixer. We do our children a deep disservice by swooping in to "save" them from normal and healthy expressions of emotion. Support them through it, yes—but making the emotion disappear? That isn't our job, and we may even be sending the message that we aren't confident in their ability to handle those emotions.

A *meltdown* is an intense and involuntary emotional response that can overwhelm a child, often triggered by sensory overload, emotional distress, or frustration. Meltdowns may last longer and take more time for the child to recover compared to *tantrums*, which tend to be shorter emotional expressions, often triggered by a child's desire for something specific, such as a toy, attention, or a particular activity. A tantrum can turn into a meltdown because once the ball of genuine emotions starts rolling, it's almost impossible for a child to stop it themselves. During a meltdown, the child may lose control of their emotions and behaviors, making it nearly impossible for them to self-regulate; and so comes our role.

I know that sometimes these big feelings can seem pretty perplexing, but they're actually linked to their developing brains. There are several reasons why these emotional outbursts are more frequent in early childhood:

- **Underdeveloped prefrontal cortex.** This part of the brain, which manages impulse control, emotional regulation, and decision-making, isn't fully mature in young kids. As a result, children can't regulate their emotions as effectively as adults, leading to more intense and rapid emotional responses.

- **Developing language skills.** Often, young children don't have the language skills to express their feelings and needs. When they're frustrated or overwhelmed, this inability to communicate can quickly escalate to a meltdown.

- **New coping skills.** Young kids are just beginning to learn how to cope with their emotions in appropriate ways. When overwhelmed by their feelings, they may default to meltdowns, unable to access the "tools" they're working on.

- **Developing sensory systems.** The sensory systems in young children are still developing, and they may be more sensitive to stimuli in their environment. This heightened sensitivity can contribute to sensory overload, making it challenging for them to process and cope with various stimuli, leading to meltdowns. Keep in mind too that the amount of meltdowns a child has are closely aligned with the inborn temperament a child has. A deeply feeling or highly sensitive child is prone to feeling things with more intensity in their nervous system. Even between my own two children, the range of what meltdowns look like between them is profoundly different. One almost never experiences a full meltdown, more often having a short tantrum, whereas the other feels their feelings intensely, deeply,

and for a long time. They each require different types of support and it's taken much learning on my part to understand and try to fulfill my role for each.

- **Myelination.** The ongoing process of myelination in young brains, which involves the development of a protective sheath around nerve fibers, affects how efficiently these nerves communicate. This can significantly impact a child's emotional regulation, as the developing brain is still learning to process and respond to emotional stimuli effectively.

- **Lack of understanding.** Young children are navigating a complex world of emotions. Without a clear understanding of these feelings, they can struggle to articulate or comprehend what they're going through, which is scary, and can lead to meltdowns.

As they grow, their brains mature, and they acquire skills in emotional regulation, language, and coping, the intensity and frequency of meltdowns typically decrease.

When a child is in such a heightened state, we have this invitation to zoom out from that moment and get curious—*compassionately curious*—about what's going on for them. It's that last straw that breaks the camel's back, as it's said, and this is often true for emotions. They build and build and build until the pressure demands to be released. You may sometimes even notice that the child is having a tough day, where nothing feels "right" to them and whining is taking over, but after they have the full emotional release of a stuck feeling in the form of tears or a meltdown, they finally feel calm.

Our role during meltdowns is all about co-regulation. Children learn to self-regulate through repeated experiences of co-regulation with adults. Regulation can't be "taught," as it's developed through experience, not just instruction. It's through consistent repeated interactions with a calm adult that children form the neural pathways needed to manage their emotions independently.

UNDERSTANDING CO-REGULATION IN THE EARLY YEARS

Co-regulation is a vital process through which you, as a parent or caregiver, help your child manage and understand their emotions and behaviors. By actively engaging with your child during moments of distress, you provide the external support they need to develop their own self-regulation skills—essentially you share your calm. To normalize this even more, think about YOU. As adults, we also seek out co-regulation. When life throws its curveballs, how often do we reach out for a comforting hug from our partner, sit down over coffee with a friend, or pick up the phone to hear our mom's voice? Rarely do we choose to face tough emotions by retreating to cry alone in our room. This instinct to seek connection is a fundamental human need, and it underscores the importance of co-regulation across all ages.

For children, co-regulation isn't just about cuddles (though those are great too!). It happens in various ways throughout the day. It could be a shared laugh that cuts through a moment of frustration, a calm voice supporting them as they learn to tie shoelaces, or even a quiet sit-down together after a minor mishap with spilled juice. Each of these moments is an opportunity to teach our kids how to manage their emotions and behaviors, mirroring the many ways adults seek and provide support in our own relationships. Co-regulation is an ongoing process, subtly woven through our daily interactions, supporting our children's emotional growth and resilience.

As we know, the most profound gift we can offer our children is the foundation of a healthy and strong attachment. This deep-rooted connection provides them with the security and confidence needed to explore and grow. True independence springs from a solid base of dependence, as we explore throughout this book. By nurturing their need for closeness and support early on, we empower them to venture into the world boldly and independently. This paradoxical truth—that to soar in independence, one must first be firmly grounded in dependable relationships—is at the heart of raising resilient and self assured humans.

Research emphasizes the importance of self-regulation skills, including patience, impulse control, and empathy, which are foundational for navigating complex social environments and personal challenges. Studies in developmental psychology suggest that children who master these skills through consistent co-regulatory interactions tend to perform better academically, have lower levels of stress, and exhibit healthier social behaviors. For example, the ability to manage impulses allows children to make thoughtful decisions and fosters resilience in frustrating situations, directly impacting their emotional and mental health.

Effective co-regulation also enhances communication between children and their caregivers (us!), laying the groundwork for more responsive and understanding relationships. This improved communication is crucial in reducing behavioral challenges, as children feel more understood and less inclined to act out to express their needs or emotions. According to research from the fields of psychology and child development, children who experience a nurturing environment where caregivers actively engage in co-regulation are more likely to develop secure attachment styles later in life. These styles are associated with positive outcomes in various areas of life, including personal relationships and professional success, demonstrating the long-term benefits of a co-regulatory approach to child-rearing.

"Many people assume that discipline is the best way to help children behave better. But co-regulation is the key to developing self regulation, which results in better behaviors as the natural end product."

—DR. MONA DELAHOOK

DEVELOPMENT OF SELF-REGULATION

It's easy to lose our cool when our kids are losing theirs, as a typical human response to someone screaming is for our nervous system to also heighten. From an evolutionary standpoint, the heightened nervous response to someone yelling, especially our own child, is tied to survival and protection. Loud noises or signs of distress would have signaled potential danger to our ancestors, prompting an immediate, alert reaction to assess threats and protect offspring. This response primes us for action—whether to soothe, escape, or confront the danger. In modern contexts, this can mean our body is preparing to handle the situation with our child, ensuring their safety and attempting to restore calmness to the environment. While you'd have been saving your child from a tiger back then, now the "threat" could very well be that broccoli was served at dinner. So, it's okay to take a moment to soothe your nervous system before responding.

If we can keep ourselves calm, we can share that calm with them. A child's nervous system can attune to our calm state through co-regulation, where our steady presence provides a model that the child instinctively mirrors. This physiological synchronization happens as the child unconsciously picks up on our calm breathing, steady voice, and relaxed body language, prompting their own nervous system to down-regulate.

Self-Regulation

DEVELOPMENT OF SELF-REGULATION

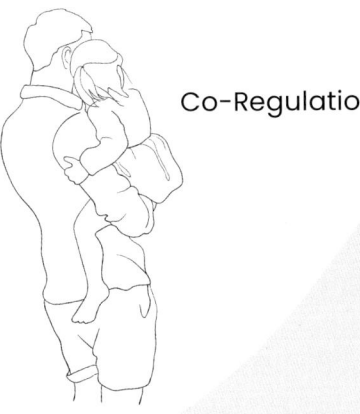

Co-Regulation

Sometimes it's enough to be near the child and simply maintain that presence of calm and empathy.

Other times, they may need more support and so, when you're ready, get down to their level; kneel or sit on the floor with them. Why? We're giants, comparably. Giants who send a primitive response to their brain that says while they're in that dysregulated mode, our big ole selves looming over them seem like more of a threat. So instead, get close and get down on their eye level. This is a sign of respect that shows them, "Hey, I get it, something is going on with you and you need more direct attention from me. I'm here." If you think about it, they're always having to look up at us and we're always looking down at them. We want to try to even that dynamic out.

During moments of dysregulation, it's difficult for your child to absorb your words, as their prefrontal cortex—their brain's command center for processing—isn't fully engaged. Instead of labeling their feelings or instructing them on how to find calm, in that exact moment, it's often more helpful to simply be present with them. That verbal guidance is helpful later on, as they've calmed down. As always, follow your child's lead. Some children do want to hear their grown-ups' calming guidance, and others really, *really* don't want to hear anything.

By modeling your calm, you show them that all is well inside of you, so that they can feel safe and understand that though it feels trying in this moment, all will be well inside of them soon, too. On the other hand, if they're in a dysregulated state, in a meltdown mode, where their nervous system is saying, "Ahh, this is an emergency! Trigger the fight, flight, freeze, fawn responses!" and then they look at us and we're yelling at them for their meltdown, it just affirms the nervous

system, saying, "Ahh, look at my parent—they're freaking out too—*this really is an emergency*!" We would rather our kids look at us and see a calm and compassionate guide ready to steer them through the "emergency," not join in panicking with them.

As the weather maker, you're their sun, shining warm light onto them in their darkest moments. You're quite magical like that. So, hold space in your calming warmth for them. No need to whip out a shiny toy to distract from the feelings; we want to show them that we believe they can work through the emotion, and distractions inhibit that practice. If your child is the kind who likes hugs at this time, then go for it. That's up to them. Some kids need to process—ride through the emotion—get much closer to the light at the end of that tunnel, *and then* accept or want physical connection.

Imagine a child's emotions like a delicate flower bud. Day by day, as you tend to this bud with co-regulation, it slowly blossoms into a sturdy flower, needing less and less care to stand tall. Your nurturing presence, love, and safety act as the sunlight and water, fostering their growth and resilience, eventually giving them the tools and confidence to thrive *without* you.

Even the most beautiful lives will feel pain, sorrow, and hardship, and we want our kids to know that while it can be hard, they can do this. They can feel *through* it. All emotions are welcome, and our job is to guide them, not fix them. Let them know their feelings are okay, even if some behaviors are not.

A note: If you're concerned about the frequency or intensity of your child's meltdowns, consulting a medical professional is always a wise step for guidance and evaluation.

NURTURING THE NERVOUS SYSTEM

Every person, big or small, has their own set of sensory needs, likes, and dislikes, and these can change based on what's happening around them or how they're feeling. It's crucial to figure out what kind of sensory input works best for you and your kids, even and especially during those tougher moments. For instance, if your child is getting antsy in a noisy, crowded place, a bear hug might help them feel more secure and less chaotic. Or maybe a few minutes on a swing will do the trick after a tough day. The key is a deeper understanding in the truth that we can't just look at behaviors as one situation, there is always more going on in the nervous system that must be uncovered.

Being aware of these sensory tools not only helps you tailor your approach to meet your child's needs in real-time, but also supports their journey toward becoming calm, content kids. Plus, it's a great way to strengthen your connection, showing them you're there and you get what they need.

We can also find our sensory *triggers*. Yep, triggers keep coming up! Like as a parent have you ever felt like if one more person touches you, you might just literally explode. Yeah, your sensory system is in overdrive. Or how about the auditory overload of hearing the TV, the oven timer beeping, a child crying, and the sink running all at the same time. That one will personally do me in. It is helpful to know this for ourselves to get ahead of things, like putting in some ear plugs! And it is also helpful to observe our own kids and see when they're having a visceral response to the input around them so that we can better support them, as well.

The sensory system is like your body's control panel, helping you figure out how to interact with the world around you. It's super important in both calming ourselves down (self-regulation) and helping others do the same (co-regulation), especially for kids who are still learning the ropes. Understanding different types of sensory input and how they can soothe or stimulate is key to managing emotions and reactions. Note too that every nervous system is unique and what feels great to one body may feel the complete opposite to another!

Some Different Types of Sensory Input:

- **Deep Pressure:** Think of how great it feels to get a firm hug or snuggle under a heavy blanket. This kind of pressure can really help chill out an overstimulated nervous system, making you feel secure and grounded. We especially love weighted blankets for this!

- **Vestibular Input:** This is all about balance and movement. Activities like swinging, rocking, or spinning help some kids feel more in control and less anxious. It's like finding calm in motion. Sensory swings are a great option here.

- **Tactile Input:** This involves anything to do with touch. Playing with different textures—smooth, scratchy, squishy—can be a great support. Also consider the potential that there is too much tactile input. Uncomfortable or itchy clothing can be a big trigger for sensitive kids.

- **Proprioceptive Input:** This refers to activities that involve muscle resistance and awareness of body position. Think climbing, jumping, or pushing against something. These actions tell your brain where your body is in space and can be really grounding.

- **Auditory Input:** For some, calming music or certain sounds can be just the trick to mellow out. Others might need a quieter environment, as too much noise can crank up the stress.

- **Visual Input:** Calming visual scenes, like watching fish swim in an aquarium or clouds drifting in the sky, can also help soothe the mind. On the flip side, clutter or bright lights might be overwhelming for some.

65

TIME-IN

The concept of co-regulation is a direct contrast to what many were, and still are, being raised on, which was usually a time-out. In modern parenting, there's a shift toward approaches like "time-in," diverging from traditional methods of secluding children until they're behaving in the way a parent desires. Time-in involves guiding and supporting a child through challenging moments within the context of a nurturing relationship. This approach prioritizes emotional regulation skills, connection, and teaching positive behaviors. It aims to maintain a strong parent–child bond even during difficult times, fostering a sense of security and trust.

On the other hand, time-out, with its focus on temporary isolation, doesn't actively teach emotional regulation and can potentially lead to negative associations with punishment. Isolation methods like this assume that children can independently reflect on and regulate their emotions without adult support, which doesn't align with their developmental stage and leaves them more confused and dysregulated than before, but trying to hide it so that they can get out of time-out. One of the big issues with this is that it can confirm a child's fear that they're not acceptable, worthy, or lovable in their family, if they're not acting in a certain desirable way. Rather than a parent/caregiver co-regulating and helping them make better choices, it's a shutting out of attention or affection until they're "acceptable."

Modern parenting research leans toward strategies that recognize a child's developmental stage, providing guidance and positive reinforcement for healthy emotional and social development.

So what does a time-in actually look like? Picture this: When a child is having a bit of a tough time, instead of banishing them to the corner, we invite them to sit nearby, usually in a calm corner, with a caring adult with them or close by. It's a chance for them to let out their feelings and eventually cool down in a safe space. Co-regulation certainly doesn't require a "Peace Corner" or a "time-in," per se, but it does help to have it as an option!

The time-in gives us the golden opportunity to connect and then, when they've calmed down, address whatever needs adjusting or learning. Why does this positive time-in business work, you ask? Well:

- It makes kids feel like their needs matter.

- We get a chance to connect with our little ones before diving into corrections.

- Kids get the space to process a whole bunch of feelings, *safely*.

- Parents don't feel like they're losing control or getting into a power struggle just to keep a child in time-out.

- Kids don't feel isolated, shamed, or scared.

- It opens up the floor for a real conversation between parents and kids about what's really going on.

PEACE CORNER

Think of this time-in as a personal space for the child. Feeling angry and needing to kick, scream, or hit something? Okay, do it in your safe space. And hey, no other humans allowed unless they're invited—a crucial guideline, especially if there are siblings in the mix.

You may need to pick up and carry a child to a space like this, so that they and others around them stay safe. If no one is in harm's way, then the child could prefer to ride through the tunnel of their emotions right where they are. Either one is okay; it's up to you to know what's right at that time. When you set up a Peace Corner, though, it's often the child who desires the calm energy of the space, and they prefer to be there when things get tough. So, how do we create a Peace Corner?

- Choose an area in the home that isn't secluded. We prefer to put ours in the same area as her books—doubling as a reading nook.

- Add pillows and any stuffed animals to make the area inviting and *safe*. We want this place to be one that they feel invited to plop their little bodies into. Soft items create a calming sensory experience.

- Using a corner (if possible) allows them a bit of a visual sensory break—as two sides are closed in—bringing some added calm to the scene.

- Adding a mirror to the space allows them to see their emotion and identify it. Ours is a handheld mirror stuck onto the side of her shelf with command strips.

- Remember, the child is free to come and go from this space as they please. With time, this becomes identified to them as a safe space to work through their emotions.

- This is a neutral space to talk about emotions and conceptualize what happened. Get down on their level, validate, process together. If a limit needed to be set, once the child has worked through the emotion—it is time to talk about our limit and its importance (without shame, blame, or guilt).

Similarly, in a Montessori classroom, you'd find the Montessori Peace Table, sometimes known as the Peace Corner. When a conflict arises between children, they're encouraged to go to the Peace Table to discuss the issue.

The idea is that the children alternate speaking and listening, often using an object like a "peace rose" to signify who has the floor, fostering active listening, empathy, and respect for diverse viewpoints. It empowers them to express themselves and collaboratively find solutions, with guidance for younger children, teaching vital communication and conflict resolution skills.

What a peaceful place this world would be if every child had the opportunity to grow up learning these skills.

PEACE EDUCATION

Similarly, in a Montessori classroom, you'd find the Montessori Peace Table, sometimes known as the Peace Corner. When a conflict arises between children, they're encouraged to go to the Peace Table to discuss the issue. The idea is that the children alternate speaking and listening, often using an object like a "peace rose" to signify who has the floor, fostering active listening, empathy, and respect for diverse viewpoints. It empowers them to express themselves and collaboratively find solutions, with guidance for younger children, teaching vital communication and conflict resolution skills.

What a peaceful place this world would be if every child had the opportunity to grow up learning these skills! And that said, Dr. Montessori was not just cultivating peace in the classroom, nor are we singularly cultivating peace in our homes. Our mission is bigger than just us.

Maria Montessori believed that education is key to achieving lasting world peace. She developed an educational model that develops peaceful individuals who understand their role in creating a harmonious world. By incorporating these practices into everyday learning, whether in the home or classroom (ideally both. Montessori education aims to nurture individuals who are not only academically capable, but also emotionally intelligent, empathetic, and committed to social justice and environmental sustainability.

Understanding this, we see how the peace corner, peaceful time-in, and peace rose are more than just "tools"; they are essential parts of a larger philosophy aimed at building a peaceful, just, and sustainable world.

As always, a visual is really helpful. Here we see Sonnie McFarland's peace flower model where each petal represents a different aspect of peace education. This flower helps us understand how all these pieces come together to create a comprehensive understanding.

- **Self-Awareness:** This is about understanding your own emotions, thoughts, and behaviors. The peace corner and peaceful time-in help children reflect on themselves and manage their feelings.

- **Community Awareness:** This involves recognizing the importance of community and your role within it. The peace rose, for example, teaches kids how their actions impact others and the importance of resolving conflicts peacefully.

- **Cultural Awareness:** Appreciating and respecting cultural diversity. Montessori classrooms often explore different global cultures and traditions, helping children see themselves as part of a larger, diverse world.

- **Environmental Awareness:** Understanding how our actions affect the environment and the importance of sustainability. Montessori education emphasizes nature-based learning and taking care of our planet.

- **Social Awareness:** Recognizing social injustices and working towards social harmony. Age appropriate discussion, our modeling, and again, using tools like peaceful time-in and the peace rose help children develop empathy and a sense of fairness from an early age.

- **Global Awareness:** Coming to understand global issues and how everything is connected. Montessori education encourages children to think globally, promoting the idea that peace in the classroom can lead to peace in the world.

As Montessorians, we know the truth in these words, "Preventing war is the work of politicians, establishing peace is the work of educationists."

—MARIA MONTESSORI

2

The Child

In these pages, we will explore the Montessori philosophy of viewing the child as a whole person deserving of respect at every level, and extending the utmost kindness we can offer by taking the time to learn more about who they are and their unique development.

THE AUTHENTIC SELF AND INNER GUIDE

According to Montessori, each child possesses an innate drive for self-construction and self-realization. She believed that children aren't blank slates waiting to be filled with information, but rather, they are active learners with their own inner directives.

Montessori coined the term *inner guide* to describe the child's intrinsic motivation and inner compass that directs their development. She proposed that children have deep wisdom that guides them toward activities and experiences that are developmentally appropriate and align with their individual needs and interests. This inner guide is seen as a dynamic force propelling the child toward self-discovery and the mastery of various skills.

Montessori's approach focuses on creating an environment that nurtures and supports the child's natural tendencies, allowing them to explore and learn in a self-directed manner. It's our role to understand, respect, and honor that inner guide of theirs, so that we don't hinder their growth into their authentic self. This approach is centered around fostering an environment that honors the child's individuality, encouraging self-directed learning, and facilitating the unfolding of their inner potential. There are some things that we must learn, unlearn, and grow into when it comes to this work, so let's dive into it all, shall we?

THE UNIQUE CHILD

Your child is beautifully their own.

There are many factors that contribute to a child's existence in this world, the way and level of intensity of which they experience things, and the type of support they need. Parenting is not a one-size-fits-all journey.

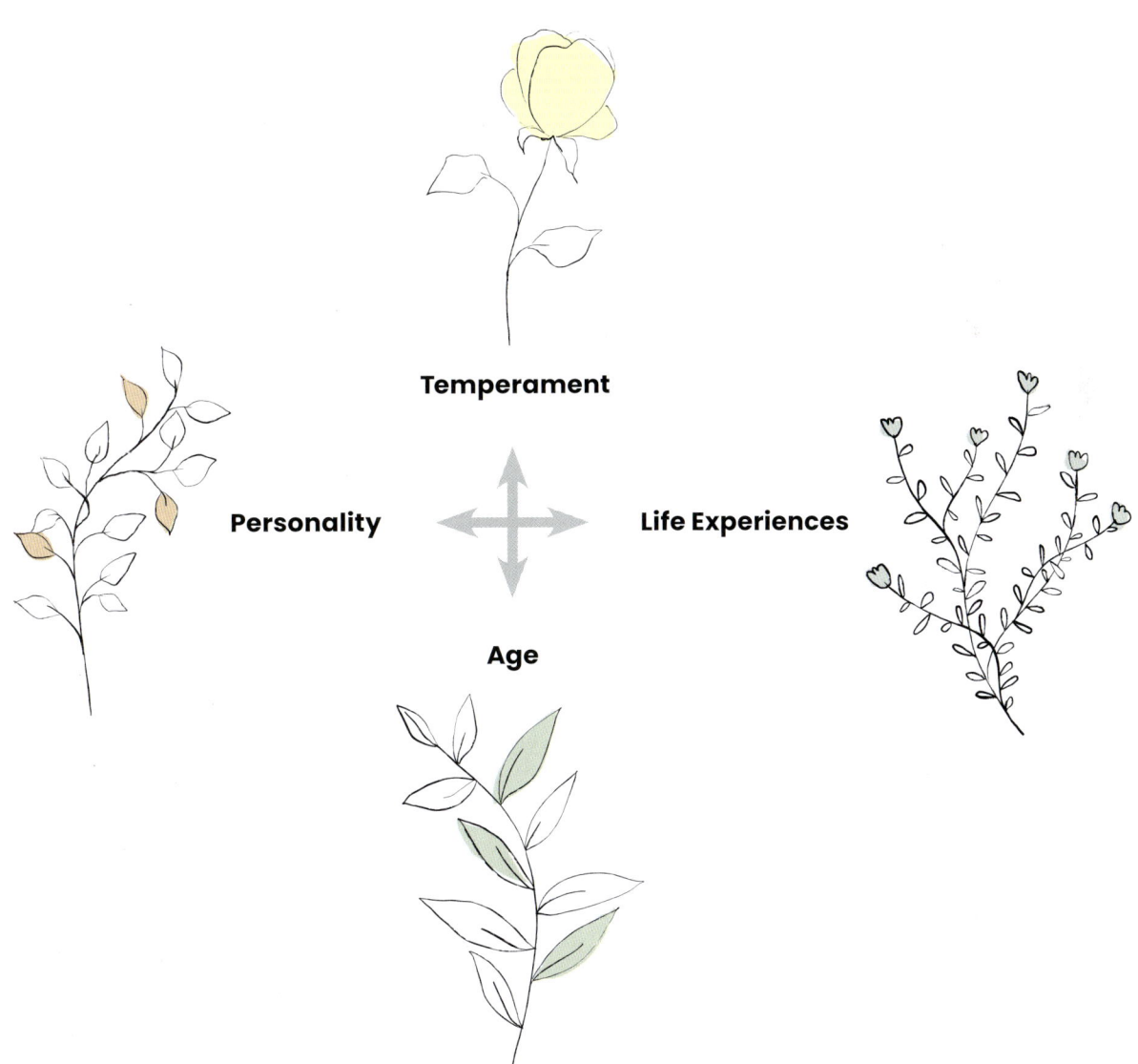

Temperament

Personality

Life Experiences

Age

Temperament refers to the inborn traits that form the foundation of a child's personality, influencing how they interact with the world around them. These traits, often evident from the earliest days, are a combination of emotional, attentional, and behavioral tendencies that remain relatively consistent throughout life. A child's temperament can greatly shape their unique life experiences and the way they need a parent to show up for them.

For instance, a child with a naturally easygoing temperament may adapt quickly to new situations, handle changes in routine with less fuss, and generally display a positive mood. Such traits can make certain aspects of parenting more straightforward, as these children might find it easier to form social connections and be more receptive to various parenting strategies. On the other hand, a child with a more intense temperament, often characterized by high emotional reactions and resistance to new experiences, invites us to adopt a more structured approach, requiring more patience and tailored strategies to support the child.

The impact of temperament extends beyond the parent–child dynamic. It influences a child's social interactions, learning experiences, and overall emotional development. For example, a highly active child might thrive in environments where they can move and explore, while a more reserved child might excel in settings that offer a sense of calm and structure. This understanding can guide parents and educators in creating supportive environments that align with each child's innate tendencies.

Temperament plays a crucial role in emotional regulation, too. Children with different temperamental qualities need varying degrees of support to learn how to effectively manage and express their emotions. Having one highly sensitive child and one easygoing child, we've seen firsthand just how differently our kids experience the world and our parenting. One child requires all the tools in our parenting toolbox and the other, by nature, is quite content to go with the flow.

Whether you see these temperament differences in your own family, between siblings, or find them notable at a playdate with friends, know that no child needs comparison to another. Some children experience the world at a level of intensity that's tough for their sensitive little nervous systems. They feel things deeply, are more porous to the environment, have a difficult time adjusting to changes, and tend to be accused of "giving a hard time" to the adults in their life. When really, they're just doing the best they can and need more support in coping with their experiences.

This is where we come to understand that peaceful Montessori parenting is a spectrum. Not every single "tool" will work for every single child, which is why it's so important to have a deep understanding of the philosophy, rooted firmly in our values and intentions, so that we can adapt as needed while still showing up for the child with unconditional love, respect, and connection. This understanding fosters an environment where children can develop to their fullest potential and securely embrace their individual nature.

THE CAPABLE CHILD

In the Montessori world, we hear the buzz of "independence" almost constantly. But what is an independent child? It seems a little contradictory at first. So let's expand. Autonomy-supportive parenting is a style that emphasizes nurturing a child's sense of self-direction and choice, while providing appropriate guidance and boundaries. This approach is supported by research, which suggests that children raised with autonomy-supportive methods exhibit higher levels of motivation, self-esteem, and stronger problem-solving skills.

Lucky for us, Montessori is incredibly autonomy-supportive. As we know, Montessori is centered around fostering independence, respect, and a nurturing environment, which are key elements in helping a child feel capable and grow into an autonomous being.

We have to keep in mind that the way we parent our children today shapes who they'll grow into one day. Oftentimes parents are raising kids in a way deeply contrary to who they hope walks in through the front door twenty years from now, as their adult child. The message so many receive from their parents in the early years is that they should be strong, confident, capable adults *one day*, but right now, in childhood, they must be obedient, pliable, and controllable. It's as if we expect an entire upbringing, building of self, and internal voice of their childhood to be forgotten and they morph into someone else upon adulthood. Quite simply, it doesn't work this way. In fact, many of these are traits developed and nearly solidified in just the first plane of development. A person's personality is said to be "set" sometime around first grade. We, mostly, remain recognizably the same person we were at age six.

"Never help a child with a task at which he feels he can succeed."

—MARIA MONTESSORI

75

A sometimes-missed aspect of the capable, independent child, is that this stems from a strong and healthy attachment to their parents. This attachment is crucial as it provides the child with a secure base from which to explore the world. It's a misconception that fostering independence means promoting detachment. In reality, a secure attachment creates a sense of safety and trust, allowing the child to venture out and explore knowing they have a safe haven to return to. It's through this initial dependence and secure attachment that a child develops the confidence to truly soar.

I've always found this story to have a profound impact on our role as parents raising capable kids. The tale is old and the source remains unknown. It goes like this:

A man found a cocoon of a butterfly. One day a small opening appeared, and he sat and watched the butterfly for several hours as it struggled to force its body through the little hole. Then it seemed to stop making any progress—it appeared stuck.

The man decided to help the butterfly, and with a pair of scissors he cut open the cocoon. As the butterfly emerged with ease, the man was surprised. It had a swollen body and small, shriveled wings. He continued to watch the butterfly, expecting that, at any moment, the wings would dry out, enlarge, and expand to support the swollen body. He hoped that in time the body would contract and the butterfly would be able to fly.

But neither happened. In fact, the butterfly spent the rest of its life crawling around with a swollen body and shriveled wings.

It was never able to fly. In his kindness and haste, the man didn't realize that the butterfly's struggle to get through the small opening of the cocoon is nature's way of forcing fluid from the body of the butterfly into its wings so that it would be ready for flight.

Sometimes struggles are exactly what we need in life. If we go through the world with someone blocking any obstacles, it'll cripple us. We wouldn't be as strong as we could have been.

And we would never fly.

In making the shift to view our children as capable beings, we choose to believe in them even when things get hard. This looks like gentle encouragement rather than swooping in to "fix" things all the time. Our role is clear in offering the child as much or as little support as is actually needed. For example, when it comes to sleep, this might look like a child who needs to be cuddled to fall asleep, but another who just needs a kiss on the head and a "goodnight." Each child has different sleep needs, and that's okay. This stands for all aspects of development and becomes a simple guide to following the child, rather than getting stuck in conflicting parenting advice from friends. Children are so unique and will require either more or less (or just different) from us, even compared to a sibling.

Guiding a child to feel capable comes from empowering them, not enabling them. While enabling involves shielding children from the outcomes of their actions or doing everything for them, empowering gives them the appropriate amount of control early on, allowing them to own their life's journey.

SIMPLICITY

An all-but-forgotten need in childhood is simplicity. In today's fast-paced and often complex world, the value of simplicity in a child's life cannot be over-stated. At its core, simplicity offers a respite from the hustle and bustle, allowing children the space and time to grow at their own pace and to cultivate their sense of self. When life is overloaded with activities, technologies, and an abundance of choices, it can become overwhelming for children. This overload often leads to a reduction in the quality of experi-ences, as the focus shifts from engagement and learning to merely keeping up.

Simplicity, on the other hand, pares life down to the essentials, promoting deeper connections with activities and people rather than a superficial skim-ming of numerous experiences. It allows children the luxury of time—time to explore, to think, to daydream, and to engage meaningfully with their surroundings. In a slow and steady childhood, they're better able to focus and fully immerse themselves into the joys of learning and playing, without the distraction of a cluttered schedule or environment. This focused engagement is crucial for developing concentration, a sense of mastery, and self-esteem.

A simple life, with free afternoons, rather than booked-up extracurriculars, can foster creativity and imagination. When not constantly directed by structured activities or screens, children find creative ways to use their time and resources. This kind of unstructured, imaginative play is essential for cognitive and emotional development. It encourages problem-solving skills, independence, and the ability to entertain oneself—qualities that are invaluable as they grow. Free time also opens up space for the magic of boredom! Which often leads to the best discoveries of all.

With fewer distractions and commitments, families can spend more quality time together, engaging in meaningful conversations and activities. This time spent together strengthens relationships and provides a sense of security and belonging, which is crucial for a child's emotional well-being.

Embracing simplicity isn't about depriving children of experiences or opportunities; it's about prioritizing the things the lessons or sports they love, carefully selecting and carving out time for that, and then opening their schedule as much as possible otherwise. Creating an environment where they can explore, learn, and grow in a more focused, calm, and connected manner is a priority we can all make space for. It's about making room for the things that truly matter—love, connection, creativity, and play—and in doing so, allowing children the space to develop into well-rounded, grounded, and self-aware people.

77

"Children need time to become themselves—through play and social interaction. If you overwhelm a child with stuff—with choices and pseudochoices— before they are ready, they will only know one emotional gesture: More!"

—KIM JOHN PAYNE, SIMPLICITY PARENTING

EVERYDAY NEUROSCIENCE

Bottom-up brain development refers to the process by which the brain develops from the most basic functions to more complex ones. In the context of early childhood emotions and regulation abilities, bottom-up development plays a crucial role.

During the early years of a child's life, the brain undergoes rapid development, with the lower, more primitive areas developing first, even before birth. I love the visual of imagining the building of these brains as the construction of a home. First goes the foundation, which of course needs to be sturdy, and protective of all that will be built upon it. These areas of the lower brain, the foundation, are responsible for basic functions such as sensory processing, motor skills, and emotional regulation. As the child grows, the construction turns to shaping rooms, and eventually wiring the electrical system, all in a specific sequence. These are when the higher-level brain regions, responsible for more advanced cognitive functions like reasoning and decision-making, begin to develop. This building continues on through adulthood. Although the brain stops growing in size by early adolescence, the teen years are all about fine-tuning how the brain works. The brain finishes developing and maturing in the mid-to-late twenties.

Early experiences, like building materials, have varying degrees of quality; the quality of a child's early experiences affects the sturdiness of that child's brain architecture. A beautiful and sturdy foundation in the early years enhances the likelihood of positive health and overall well-being outcomes later in life, while a weaker foundation may pose challenges. The good news is that it's never too late to support strong brain development.

The impact on early childhood emotions and regulation abilities is significant. The lower brain areas, including the limbic system, which is associated with emotions, develop early on. This means that young children experience emotions intensely and more instinctively. They react emotionally to situations before fully understanding or processing them cognitively. In other words, going from zero to one hundred happens in the blink of an eye, without their conscious control. So when you're looking at your precious little one who just asked for cereal and then took one bite and threw it across the room crying in rage that it didn't taste how they expected—know that this is a lower brain, emotional response that flooded them before reasoning could catch up.

As a result of all this slow brain building, young children rely on us to help them regulate their emotions. We nurture and care for their nervous systems, until one day, they're able to care for their own.

I love the visual of imagining the building of these brains as the construction of a home.

EMERGING SKILLS

You may see your toddler take a bite of cereal that didn't taste how they expected and say, "No thank you, Daddy," calmly, without throwing it across the room, screaming in rage. That doesn't mean that they'll be able to pull out that regulation and reasoning every time. Development isn't linear, which is pretty darn hard to remember as a parent! Just because our child can do something one day—whether it's polite responses to breakfast, putting on shoes with ease, or saying goodbye without a blink at drop-off—it doesn't mean they can access that regulation or those skills all the time.

Every day, new emerging skills are popping up, and in this nonlinear development, the child's abilities can change by the hour. We've all heard the concept of regressions, for instance, where suddenly the child is unable to do something they've been doing for some time. Regression refers to a temporary backward shift in behavior, skills, or developmental milestones. It's a perfectly normal part of child development, and can also be a response to stress, change, or challenges that a child is facing. Common triggers for regression in children include major life changes, such as the birth of a sibling, parental separation, starting a new school, or experiencing trauma. It's essential for caregivers and parents to respond with understanding and support during these periods, as regression is usually a temporary and adaptive coping mechanism for the child to navigate challenging circumstances.

Even further, we can consider this not a stepping backward in their development, but more so a stepping aside to make room for other things. Whether it's to make room for the emotional capacity needed to process a challenge or for the child to focus on another new skill, there's usually some sort of progression going on, and what an incredible thing that is.

One of the tricky things with understanding emerging skills, paired with the big talk of independence, is that kids sometimes just need help. It may be true that they *can* put their shoes on, yet are asking mom to help with the shoes—not because they aren't able, but because we all just need some extra love sometimes. I'll sometimes ask the child whether what they actually need is help with their shoes, or if it is some connection they're needing. I may sit next to them, give a hug, or ask if they need the "one finger helper," which is exactly what it sounds like. Instead of just taking over putting their shoes on for them, we can ask exactly where they need help from our one finger. They'll show you where the tricky part is—maybe the heel is bending in as they try to slide the shoe on, and you'll support them there with your one finger rather than taking over completely. In this act, you've shown them just how little your role was—only one tiny finger—and they've done the rest themselves, which maintains their confidence and promotes more likelihood that they'll take on the task themselves next time.

THE ABSORBENT MIND

Maria Montessori's concept of the *absorbent mind* in early childhood refers to the unique ability of young children to effortlessly soak up and internalize information from their environment. According to Montessori, during the first six years of life, what she calls *The First Plane of Development,* children have a mind that's highly receptive to learning and assimilating knowledge. This period is divided into two sub-phases: the unconscious absorbent mind (from birth to around age three) and the conscious absorbent mind (from around age three to six).

During the unconscious absorbent mind phase, children absorb information from their surroundings without conscious effort. They effortlessly acquire language, motor skills, and cultural knowledge simply by being exposed to their environment. Montessori emphasized the importance of providing a rich, stimulating, and orderly environment during this stage.

In the conscious absorbent mind phase, which corresponds with the preschool and early elementary years, children actively engage in purposeful learning. They become more aware of their surroundings and deliberately seek out knowledge through exploration and hands-on experiences. Montessori educational materials are designed to cater to the absorbent mind, fostering self-directed learning and allowing children to explore and understand various concepts at their own pace.

Montessori believed that recognizing and nurturing the absorbent mind's capabilities during these formative years is crucial for a child's holistic development and lays the foundation for a lifelong love of learning.

"The child has a different relation to his environment from ours. . . . the child absorbs it. The things he sees aren't just remembered; they form part of his soul. He incarnates in himself all in the world about him that his eyes see and his ears hear."

—MARIA MONTESSORI

81

FOUR DEVELOPMENTAL DOMAINS

In the world of your child's development, developmental domains are like the different gears that drive a child's growth engine. These domains are the various aspects of a child's overall development, encompassing physical, cognitive, social/emotional, and language. It's helpful to consider each domain and get curious about if needs are getting met throughout when we're faced with challenges. One of my biggest reminders to parents is that when we feel challenged by our child's behavior, it may be time to challenge them—in the best ways, that is!

Physical Development

The first developmental domain is the body's grand adventure—fine and gross motor skills, coordination, and the physical evolution from reflexively wrapping their little hands around your finger to crawling to conquering the playground monkey bars.

We're physical beings who all need movement in our lives, and from the womb on, our little ones are constantly growing and mastering new physical skills.

Honoring the natural physical development of the child requires *freedom of movement*. Maria Montessori observed that young children have an innate drive to explore and interact with their environment actively. In fostering freedom of movement, we recognize the interconnectedness of physical and cognitive development. Movement becomes a means for children to absorb knowledge from their environment actively; as Montessori said, "Watching a child makes it obvious that the development of his mind comes about through his movements." The child's self-directed exploration is seen as a natural and essential part of the learning process, which is why you see children moving about through a Montessori classroom, rather than sitting still at desks all day. Through movement, children not only develop their bodies, but also refine their senses, enhance concentration, and build a foundation for future academic and life skills.

According to Montessori (and modern-day research), unrestricted movement supports the development of fine and gross motor skills, coordination, spatial awareness, and balance.

We design the home to encourage purposeful movement, with carefully chosen materials and furniture accessible to children at their height, promoting a sense of independence and responsibility. In a Montessori home, you'll typically find a child-sized table and chairs for the kids to come and eat at, rather than always using a highchair; a balance of child-led walks versus always seated stroller rides; and freedom from walkers and jumpers, so that the child can follow their natural progression of movement and abilities. This too is the safest way to develop, as spending excessive time in containers can impact the natural development of muscles and bones.

While we respect the child's need to move and explore their bodies, we also need to keep them safe, because there's a big difference between a healthy dose of "risky play" compared to dangerous play. For example, a child who climbs up onto the table isn't a defiant child; this is a child who's showing a need to climb. Yet the table is both not safe to climb on, nor is it showing respect to the environment. Rather than simply telling a child, "*No climbing!*" we would approach this with something like, "Oh wow, you want to climb! I see that. The table isn't safe to climb on. I'll help you down and we'll go try the Pikler triangle," being sure to physically help them follow through with the boundary you set. This is why you'll find climbing apparatus in a Montessori home. Not every family has the space or means to invest in a Pikler triangle, but there are many found second-hand and also tons of great options for safe climbing without one! You may pull down the couch cushions, look for a good climbing tree outside, or head to the park.

When you see a child pushing furniture throughout the house, dragging heavy items, lifting chairs, etc., this might look like a frustrating behavior, but it's a sign that they need some heavy work challenge! "Heavy work" is a term that refers to activities that involve the pushing/pulling of the muscle joints within our bodies. These activities create resistance input to the muscles and this feedback helps to calm and regulate a child's nervous system. We add felt tabs to the bottom of the child-sized furniture and our kitchen

82

chairs, so that the kids can move them about in this type of work. In toddlerhood, I offer a sealed gallon jug of water for the little ones to move back and forth to get that great integration in!

If we're seeing chaotic roughhousing—you know the moments when it just looks like those little nervous systems are disorganized and they're at risk of hurting themselves or others—then it may be time to offer an obstacle course challenge! Rather than telling the child to just stop and sit still (which has never helped in the history of ever), offer an opportunity for them to organize that nervous system through an obstacle course—the right kind of challenge to get the input their body needs, in a safe way. Crash pad, balancing, crawling, spinning—help the child focus on a task, find success, and get the sensory input needed to move the energy through them rather than kept stuck inside them.

Getting creative and curious about the child's physical and sensory world is key to uncoding so many needs and behaviors!

"One of the most important practical aspects of our method has been to make the training of the muscles enter into the very life of the children so that it is intimately connected with their daily activities. Education in movement is thus fully incorporated into the education of the child's personality."

—MARIA MONTESSORI,
THE DISCOVERY OF THE CHILD

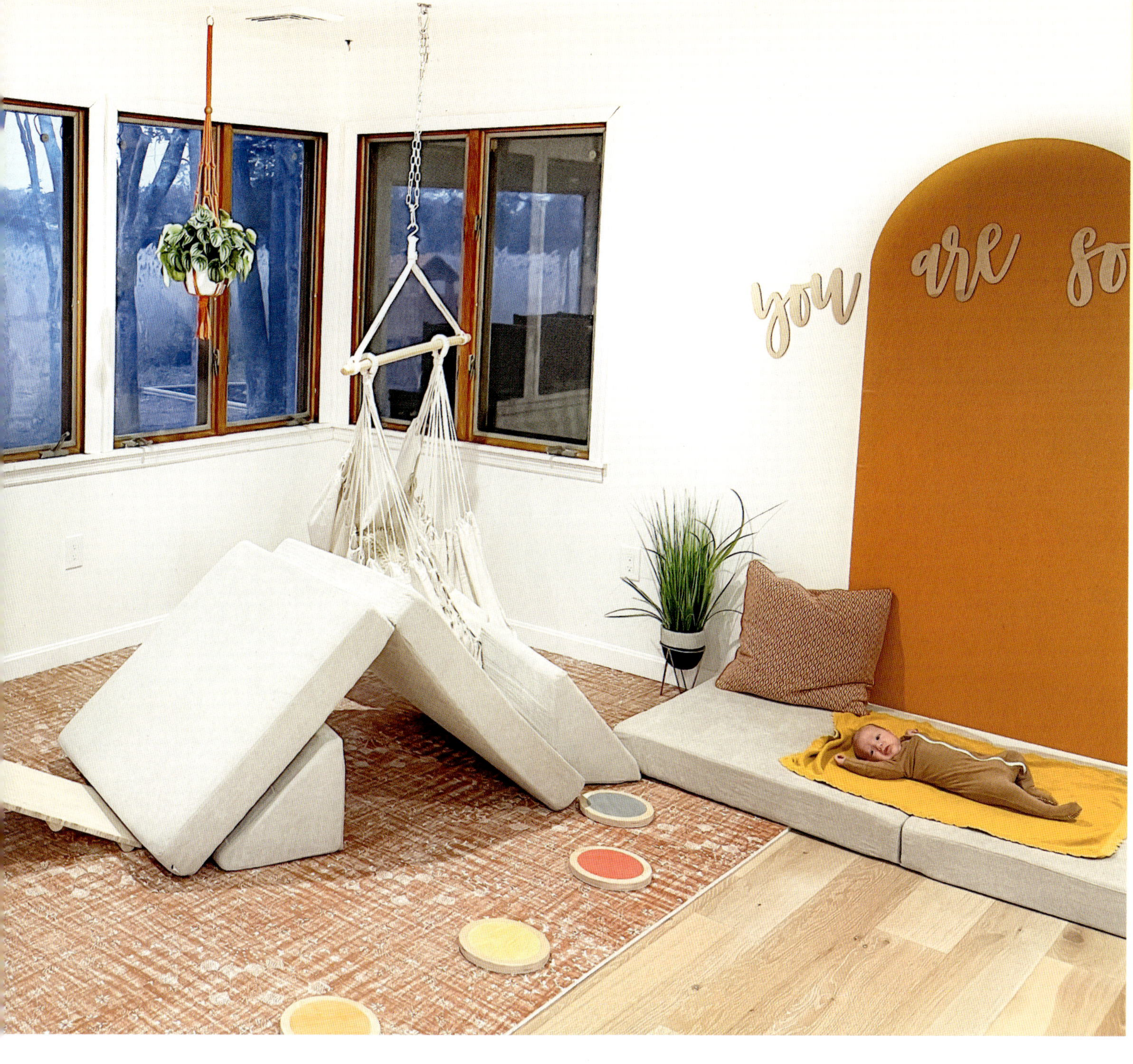
you are so

Cognitive Development

There's this magical place in learning new things where the child can feel challenged, yet succeed. Through observation we can offer work that's just right—the sweet spot.

For instance, we wouldn't offer a child a twenty-four-piece puzzle if they haven't yet mastered a twelve-piece—and a four- to six-piece puzzle before that, and a two-piece before that! When we offer materials far above their abilities, a few things happen: they lose confidence, they give up quickly, or they ask us to do it for them. By making sure that what we offer is appropriate, we help them build confidence, foster greater concentration skills, and grow in autonomy.

So many circuits are still awaiting connection in those brilliant brains. For anyone, adults included, constantly feeling like you're failing will bring up a lot of feelings: frustration, sadness, low self-esteem. So how do we boost their confidence with a challenge and get those longer strides of independent play that so many Montessorians talk about? Well, your best bet is to be sure you're offering the right kind of work.

"The child should love everything that he learns, for his mental and emotional growths are linked. Whatever is presented to him must be made beautiful and clear, striking his imagination. Once this love has been kindled, all problems confronting the educationalist will disappear."

—MARIA MONTESSORI

86

A great starting point before introducing any new work for your child is isolating skills and scaffolding along the way.

Let's use this easy DIY work to demonstrate what this looks like:

Say the goal is working on this bead sorting work.

This work would be appropriate for a toddler up to age six and up, as there is potential for extensions of learning over and over again.

All of this is going on with just a simple work, like bead sorting:

Fine Motor Skills:

- *Pincer Grip*: Using fingers to pick up and manipulate small beads enhances the pincer grip, an essential fine motor skill.
- *Hand-Eye Coordination*

Cognitive Skills:

- *Color Recognition*
- *Pattern Recognition*

Mathematical Concepts:

- *Counting*
- *Matching and Grouping*

Language Skills:

- *Vocabulary Development*: Discussing colors, shapes, and patterns during the activity supports language development.
- *Following Instructions*

Social Skills:

- *Cooperation*: Engaging in bead sorting as a small group/sibling work encourages teamwork, promoting social skills.

Sensory Exploration:

- *Tactile Sensitivity*: Handling beads of different textures enhances tactile sensitivity and sensory exploration.
- *Visual Discrimination*: Differentiating between beads based on visual characteristics contributes to visual discrimination skills.

Problem-Solving:

- *Critical Thinking*: Figuring out how to sort beads based on given criteria or creating patterns involves critical thinking.

Emotional Development:

- *Patience*: Engaging in tasks that require careful sorting fosters patience and concentration.

See, there's so much going on!

A great place to start is scooping, strengthening the palmar grasp (fig. 1).

Then, move to isolating that pincer grip and practicing simply picking up the beads and transferring them into another cup (fig. 2).

And then attempt to slide them on the skewer (fig. 3).

They'd also need to have exposure and practice with identifying colors. By finding success with the first skills, they gain confidence to approach the next step, when ready—which could be in hours, days, weeks, or months! We can get creative about adjusting their work to meet the level of development they're at.

Alfred Adler believed that behavior issues were often manifestations of an individual's efforts to cope with feelings of inferiority. Maria Montessori knew that by offering that sweet spot in work, where the child can feel challenged yet eventually succeed, they feel good about themselves, and we see a much more peaceful child.

Social/Emotional Development

Covering everything from regulation skills, to making friends, understanding social cues, and playing cooperatively, emotional development deals with how kids understand and manage their emotions. From the highs of joy to the lows of a bumped knee, it's all part of the emotional journey. Likewise, the resilience needed to face those challenges in learning and continue on would be fostered here.

Knowing all you know about brain development now, a lot of this makes more sense, right? Just as we wouldn't punish a child for having difficulty in their math work, we wouldn't punish a child for having difficulty in social or emotional challenges. We would support them and teach new skills. Everything from learning to identify emotions in themselves and others to saying hello to a friend upon arrival are skills to be learned.

The ability to identify and understand emotions, for example, is a foundational skill that impacts children's social interactions, learning abilities, personal development, and mental health. Some key benefits:

- **Emotional Regulation:** Manages feelings effectively.

- **Empathy Development:** Fosters compassion and understanding.

- **Improved Communication:** Enhances clarity in expressing feelings.

- **Academic Success:** Boosts concentration and learning.

- **Healthy Relationships:** Aids in social interactions and conflict resolution.

- **Self-Awareness:** Promotes personal growth and confidence.

- **Resilience:** Strengthens ability to handle stress and setbacks.

- **Mental Health:** Supports emotional well-being.

The Zones of Regulation, modified for young kids, is a great learning tool for this! The Zones of Regulation is a framework used to teach self-regulation and emotional control. It categorizes states of alertness and emotions into four colored zones, as shown in the Wheel of Emotions. We can talk about these colored zones to help our little ones to understand:

1. **Blue Zone:** Associated with low states of alertness and down feelings such as sadness, tiredness, boredom, or feeling sick. A child in the Blue Zone may appear lethargic, withdrawn, or disinterested.

2. **Green Zone:** Signifies a calm state of alertness. It's associated with feelings of happiness, focus, and readiness to learn. Children in the Green Zone are often described as content, calm, and feeling okay or satisfied. They are in an optimal state for learning and interacting socially.

3. **Yellow Zone:** Represents a heightened state of alertness and elevated emotions, but the child still has some control. It includes feelings like frustration, excitement, silliness, nervousness, or worry. Children in the Yellow Zone may appear agitated, restless, or overly energetic.

4. **Red Zone:** Indicates an intensely heightened state of alertness and intense emotions. Emotions in the Red Zone could include anger, rage, terror, or panic. A child in the Red Zone may be out of control, have trouble thinking clearly, or be unable to make rational decisions.

Understanding these zones help kids recognize and articulate how they feel, leading to better self-regulation and emotional control. It's important to note that all zones are natural and okay to experience; the key is teaching children strategies to move between zones effectively. We also want to keep in mind that not until the end of the first plane of development, around age five and up, do kids begin to understand that we can feel multiple emotions at once. This makes processing and moving through challenging experiences very tricky for them. We might say things to help build this understanding, like, "I'm feeling nervous and excited about work today. I'm feeling two things at the same time. I wonder if that ever happens for you?"

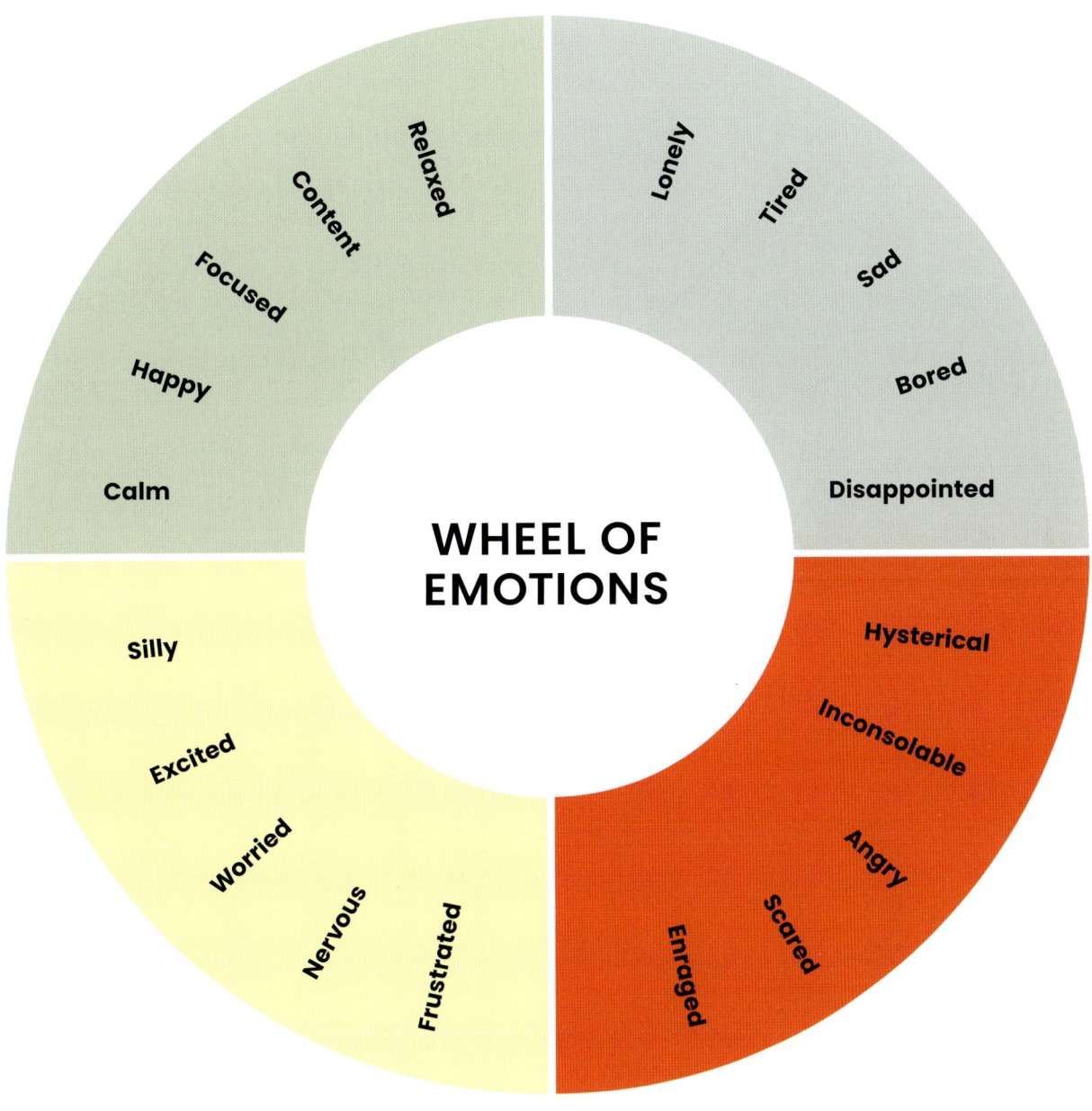

WHEEL OF EMOTIONS

Relaxed
Content
Focused
Happy
Calm

Lonely
Tired
Sad
Bored
Disappointed

Silly
Excited
Worried
Nervous
Frustrated

Hysterical
Inconsolable
Angry
Scared
Enraged

All Feelings Are Welcome, Real, and Valid

Feelings, in their essence, are neither right, wrong, good, nor bad; they are simply a reflection of our inner state. Acknowledging and accepting our emotions is an integral part of developing emotional intelligence. Of course, it's also about guiding children to express those emotions in appropriate ways. As Dr. Aliza Pressman, developmental psychologist, says, "All feelings are welcome, all behaviors are not."

It's crucial to recognize that understanding and validating emotions is just one part of the journey—a very important one though! When children feel that their emotions are acknowledged and respected, it builds a foundation of trust and secure attachment with their caregivers. This validation is crucial in developing their emotional intelligence, helping them understand and label their feelings, and enhancing their ability to empathize with others. It also encourages them to express themselves, fostering effective communication and teaching them that their voice matters. This acceptance of their emotions significantly contributes to a positive self-image and a sense of self-worth, affirming that they are valued. Additionally, understanding and acknowledging their emotions is essential in teaching children how to navigate challenges and develop resilience. They learn that it's normal to experience a range of emotions and that with support, they can overcome difficulties, building essential problem-solving skills.

It's also true that when our kids see us able to accept and hold space for their emotions, they can then feel safe to accept and hold space for their own emotions. When parents are constantly telling kids that they are overreacting, being "too much" or dramatic, the child internalizes a message that they aren't safe to feel these feelings and they're not likable when they're experiencing certain emotions, and will do everything they can to push those feelings down. We, again, want them to feel safe and capable of experiencing the whole range of emotions. We as humans are meant to "feel all the feels," as our emotions can be protective and give us vital informa-tion about our experiences.

For example, we cry in response to intense emotions like sadness, frustration, joy, and laughter. Cortisol and adrenaline are released in the tears! Seriously. Tears release stress and help us feel better.

Anger is what many consider a secondary emotion, acting as a protective response when a boundary is violated. We can teach our kids that anger shows up as a bodyguard to protect the underlying emotions of sadness, shame, fear, or guilt. Anger tells us something doesn't feel right and gives us clues as to what's going on inside of us.

By helping our kids understand that emotions have reasons and value, we help them feel safe through it. When feelings come in our home, we sing this same song (shown on page 93), ever since our kids were teeny tiny—not every single time, but when it feels appropriate and helpful based on feedback from the child.

Seeing my daughter sing this to her little brother, herself, her friends, and even sometimes to us, her parents, is the most beautiful reflection that these aren't just words to her. She's growing into a person who truly believes and is soothed by the way emotions safely move through us like waves.

As Mister Rogers said, "People have said 'Don't cry' to other people for years and years, and all it has ever meant is, 'I'm too uncomfortable when you show your feelings: Don't cry.' I'd rather have them say, 'Go ahead and cry. I'm here to be with you.'"

What would a generation of children who are secure with their emotions and have healthy coping skills look like in the world? It would be world-changing in the most incredible ways. And you are part of this movement. That's no small thing!

*"Feelings come and
feelings go
All are welcome here
It's okay to cry
It's okay to be sad
You are safe and loved
Feelings come and
feelings go
All are welcome here
It's okay to cry
It's okay to be sad
Feelings come, feelings go
And I'll always love you"*

LANGUAGE DEVELOPMENT

Understanding and using language, from those adorable first words to crafting complex sentences to writing and reading, all make up the longest of the Sensitive Periods (more on this soon) in Montessori, spanning from birth to age six. Absorbing language happens naturally through conversation, reading books, songs, playing, and much more, though we can do our best to support their development with rich language experiences. The child is drawn to your voice, lip movements, and soaks in our words like a sponge. They want to know the names of everything in the world, love hearing rhymes, singing, and are intrigued by complicated pronunciations.

Learning to express their thoughts, ideas, preferences, and feelings to reveal more about who they are is such a joy for both child and parent. The child is so eager to join in actually that it can also be a big source of frustration and that's important to acknowledge. The range at which children learn to speak varies based on many factors, and while one child may be able to pronounce words with clarity, another may be struggling at every interaction with a parent saying, "HUH?" over and over again. This is why we absolutely need to consider language barriers as a source of emotional distress in those early childhood years. Knowing this, we can get creative in the ways we support them and ease that frustration!

Boosting language in toddlers can be approached with some simple yet effective strategies. Here are a few tips:

- **Consistent Communication:** Narrate your activities, describe what you're doing, and engage in simple conversations. This intentional approach is crucial for language development.

- **Reading Together:** Read to your child daily. Choose age-appropriate books with lots of pictures and simple text. Encourage them to point at and name objects in the book.

- **Labeling the Environment:** Place labels on objects around the house, like bins for "shoes," "snacks," "shirts," etc. This helps children associate words with their corresponding objects, enhancing their vocabulary. We also find it very helpful to have the space organized and supportive in this way for children in those moments where you just don't know what they're saying. After I've already asked the child to repeat the word once, I then say, "Can you please show me?" and offer my hand to be led to what they are wanting rather than increasing their frustration by requesting multiple repeats of the word.

- **Sing Songs and Nursery Rhymes:** Songs and rhymes aren't only fun but also rhythmic and repetitive, which can help with language learning. Encourage your toddler to sing along.

- **Use Simple, Clear Language:** When speaking to your toddler, use simple sentences and speak clearly. This makes it easier for them to understand and mimic your speech.

- **Encourage Imitation:** Toddlers learn a lot by imitating. Use gestures along with words and encourage them to mimic you. This can include waving goodbye, clapping, or simple sign language.

- **Play Interactive Games:** Engage in games that involve naming objects, like puzzles with pictures and words, or simple "I Spy" games. This kind of interactive play can boost language skills.

Seek professional support if concerned. If you have concerns about your child's language development, consult with a pediatrician or a speech-language therapist for personalized advice and strategies.

Remember, every child develops at their own pace, so it's important to be patient and supportive throughout their language learning journey.

The Montessori Three-Period Lesson

The Montessori Three-Period Lesson is an amazing foundational teaching approach used to introduce and reinforce concepts and words in a clear, step-by-step manner. This method is particularly effective for vocabulary building, as it focuses on both the comprehension (understanding the word) and production (being able to say the word) aspects of language learning.

> "The more we cut away useless words, the more perfect will become the lesson."
>
> —MARIA MONTESSORI, THE MONTESSORI METHOD

The three periods are as follows:

- **Introduction or Naming (First Period):** In this phase, we introduce a new concept or object to the child, typically by saying, "This is..." For example, when introducing a geometric shape, the teacher might say, "This is a circle," while tracing the circle with a finger. The focus here is on exposing the child to the new term or concept without expecting them to recall or say it.

- **Association or Recognition (Second Period):** This period involves asking the child to recognize and identify the object or concept that was introduced. The teacher might say, "Where's the circle?" or "Please pass me the circle." This step reinforces recognition and understanding, as the child has to select the correct item from among others. It's more interactive and ensures that the child has made the correct association. This invites a conversation on the reminder to "teach by teaching, not by correcting," as Montessori said. If the child, for example, passes a square instead of a circle, we might say, "Oh, you're showing me a square. Thank you!" without saying, "Noooo, that's not a circle." We've given them both an invitation to try again and *taught* that this is a square, preserving confidence and keeping the learning joyful.

- **Recall (Third Period):** Finally, the child is asked to recall and name the object or concept on their own. The guide points to the object and asks, "What is this?" This step considers the child's memory and understanding of the concept or object. It's important that this step is only introduced when the child is ready and shows confidence in the previous step to ensure success and avoid discouragement.

The Montessori Three-Period Lesson is truly a cornerstone of the Montessori approach and can be used in such versatile ways, organically, throughout your days.

CONNECTION-BASED ACTIVITIES

These are just small moments to include in your day that increase connection and feelings of significance in the home. I keep these in my back pocket; some we do daily, and others I pull out when I notice we're just a bit off.

High, Low, Buffalo

This is an all-time favorite daily bedtime ritual in our family. Consider what time of day would feel best for your family, maybe at dinner time or after school—just aim for a moment when your little one typically seems open to communication. Each family member shares specific parts of their day to increase connection:

- High: Something that happened during the day that brought joy

- Low: Something that was hard or upsetting

- Buffalo: A random thing! We make this a silly thing, but it can be anything they want to add

Kindness Hide & Seek

This is a major love booster for little kids. We want our kids to "catch" us saying wonderful things about them! You'll start out with the usual hide and seek game, counting to ten or twenty with your eyes closed, while they run and hide. When it's time for you to search for them, you'll call out, "Oh, Asher, where are you!? I miss you so much! I miss that beautiful little voice and all your giggles! I miss your hugs and how kind you are! I miss you telling me about dinosaurs and rainbows." You can be as specific as you want to be, but the point is that you take the time to intentionally point out things that you are just so in love with about them. When you find them, your heart is going to just melt seeing how much love is beaming out of their little faces from the kindness you spoke about them. You can take turns and oftentimes they want to say kind things about the next person who's hiding! It's such a lovefest game.

Love Chase

This is done with two adults—maybe it's mom and dad, or dad and grandpa, just two people who love the child and are ready to have some fun with them. The game will have to be explained and approved by the child, as it does involve being "caught" with a hug. If they don't feel comfortable consenting to that, it's okay to just chase and omit the hug! This is a fun spin on the usual game of chase, where both adults are running after the little one saying, "No, I want to hug her first! I love her most, me me me!" and the other adult says, "No! Me! I love her more, I'm going to get that hug! I love her so much!"

Imagine being a child who has their adults running after them, thinking about how big their love is for them. What a magical time for your little one. My daughter reminds us as she's in our arms, bursting with smiles, that we can both love her so much and that's okay since she has a giant heart for everyone's love, too—totally melts our hearts.

97

Make a Family Slogan

You'll be pulling from those core values of yours to come up with a family name or "slogan." It seems like a small thing, but has a profound impact on the developing mind of a child trying to understand who they are in the world. If everyone has the same last name, or one you feel comfortable using, you can add that to the slogan. For us, we're the "Turner Helpers" as decided by my then-three-year-old. You can take the last name out and just use the word "family" or "team"—whatever feels right to you!

In organic moments of kindness like holding the door for someone, letting someone with fewer items go ahead of us, offering a dandelion to a child who fell at the park, etc. we remind ourselves of how these moments define us. We whisper to each other with a wink, "Turner Helpers strike again!" it's just the right bit of cornball-ness and adorableness that reminds them that they come from a family who tries their best to add good into the world!

Kindness Missions

Every week, since my first was a toddler, we go on kindness missions. They can be grand gestures or tiny moments of kindness. Sometimes it's planned, and sometimes we just find ourselves on a kindness mission by chance! Spreading joy, noticing the happiness you can bring to others, and how you can feel that joy inside yourself too, is one of the first builders of empathy in kids. In our family, kindness is a core value and so these missions became a way that I can show them why it matters and the impact even just one person can have on the world around them. Here are some of our Kindness Missions:

- Making cards and mailing them to friends or family
- Bringing flowers to surprise a friend who needs some cheering up
- Making cookies and dropping off to a loved one
- Picking fruits and veggies from the garden for neighbors
- Dropping off donations to the women's shelter (choose the right location for you)

We're also sure to have kindness missions for ourselves sometimes. One time we went out and picked nail polish to paint our nails and have our own little spa day. I called it a "kindness mission" because kids (and grown-ups) should know that being kind to themselves is important, too.

NERVOUS SYSTEM STATES FOR PLAY AND CONNECTION

Struggling with playing as a parent is more common than you might think. Play is most effective when we're relaxed and feeling safe, thanks to our parasympathetic nervous system. This is when we can rest, digest, and engage in play. But for many parents, the stresses of daily life keep them in a state of alertness, driven by the sympathetic nervous system's fight-or-flight mode, making it hard to immerse in playful activities with their kids.

The challenges of adult life, including distractions and unresolved trauma from our own childhoods, can make it tough to be fully present and dive into imaginative, child-led play. Recognizing this, it's beneficial for parents to find ways to relax and set aside stressors, even temporarily. It's about creating moments of connection through play by consciously setting aside time for enjoyable activities that strengthen the bond between parent and child and build happy memories.

It's also important to find the type of play that resonates with you. Play doesn't have to fit a single mold. For instance, my husband and I have different play styles—his is physical and active, while mine is more about reading, cooking, and art. The key is to engage in play that feels right for you. Genuine connection happens when you're enjoying the activity too.

Remember, play can be a form of meditation that benefits your nervous system. And it's not about playing for your child (coming up with ideas, dictating play, setting up constant activities); we let them take the lead on this to support independent play and avoid their reliance on us for play ideas. By understanding these aspects, you can release any guilt over not enjoying certain types of play and focus on creating meaningful, enjoyable play experiences that work for you and your child.

Rough and Tumble Play

Engaging in rough and tumble play with young children comes with a multitude of benefits. This type of play isn't just about letting off steam; it plays a crucial role in a child's physical, emotional, and social development. They develop coordination, balance, and motor skills as they navigate movements like rolling, tumbling, and gentle wrestling.

Beyond the physical aspects, rough and tumble play also contributes to emotional regulation. Children learn to understand and manage their own strength, gauge others' reactions, and establish boundaries. It helps them develop a sense of empathy and cooperation, building social skills, as they navigate the give-and-take nature of this play. It provides an opportunity for children to practice communication, cooperation, and negotiation. Through shared laughter and physical interaction, they build connections and strengthen relationships with peers, siblings, or parents. The impact of rough play is said to be the perfect place of *trust,* regulation, a little bit heightened "fear" (like the fear/nervous/excited feeling when playing tag and you don't want to get caught . . . Ya know?), which lays the groundwork for tons of neural connections to be made. Research by Dr. Karyn Purvis shows that while normally 400 repetitions are needed to form a new brain synapse, doing it through play (any type of play) can reduce this to just ten to twenty repetitions.

Parents can rest assured that, when supervised and within safe boundaries, rough and tumble play is a natural and beneficial part of childhood. It's a joyful and interactive way for children to learn about their bodies, emotions, and relationships with others. So, don't be afraid to join in the fun, let loose, and enjoy these playful moments with your child!

INVITING COLLABORATION

The Montessori approach is about preparing, inviting, and offering opportunities, not demanding. This requires us to be flexible, adjust our expectations, and understand that involvement is more important than perfection. Demands trigger resistance, not just in parent–child relationships, but universally, as brain science shows. This means when someone tells you to do something, a little ping in the brain goes off to say, "No! I control my own life." We're autonomous beings who want agency—kids and adults alike. As adults, we can understand when things must be done, and therefore can calm that little voice (most of the time), but kids are often overwhelmed by impulses stronger than their developing self-control, so expecting them to be "unreasonable" is actually reasonable. If we anticipate this and not let it shock us, we're more likely to handle the situation with appropriate, proactive tools.

By keeping things casual and pressure-free, we're more likely to see smooth collaborative moments. It's like the Chinese finger trap; the more you pull, the tighter it gets. But when you calmly lean in and gently pull back, the tension releases. So, we need to be intentional about our language, environment, and consistency, as we hold these boundaries around cooperative activities like brushing teeth, getting dressed and more. Let's uncover that in the pages to come!

"Raise your words, not voice. It is rain that grows flowers, not thunder."

—RUMI

101

RHYTHM & ROUTINE

Imagine embarking on a trip to Paris, but there's a twist: The entire trip is a guided group tour, and though you're trying to learn the language, you are nowhere near fluent. Initially, it seems manageable. You anticipate having visual maps and a tour guide with some skill in your language. A little patience and meeting in the middle doesn't seem too challenging. However, the scenario quickly changes when your tour guide provides no outline for the day. You start by meeting the guide for a leisurely breakfast in the hotel lobby, but then, abruptly, you're instructed to head out for a day trip. The uncertainty begins when you realize they packed your bags for you (which is odd and also unsettling, because what if they brought the itchy "extra" sweater instead of your favorite one?), and more importantly, you realize you have no idea where you're headed.

Attempts to communicate with the guide are futile due to the language barrier and the rushing about—plus the comforting visuals and maps you anticipated are absent. You hop onto the bus and eventually arrive at the Eiffel Tower (yay!), but your experience is marred by anxiety and strict group guidelines, limiting your ability to explore. Just as you begin to embrace the moment and enjoy the stunning view from the top, you're, again, abruptly told it's time to leave. Now you're off to some other undisclosed location. This lack of communication and unpredictability makes what could have been an exciting adventure into a stressful and disorienting experience, underscoring the importance of clear guidance and respect for one's plans in any journey.

This brings us to the importance of routine or rhythm charts in parenting. And while your child has an overall sense of safety with you as their grown-up, unlike the imaginary tour guide you barely knew in Paris, the parallels still remain. Kids deserve to be prepared, have predictability, and feel the comfort of structure in their days—closing that expectation gap we spoke about earlier. While the idea of a routine might seem daunting to those who prefer a more spontaneous life, research indicates that the predictability of a daily routine significantly reduces stress for children. Routines provide a sense of consistency and security, essential for their well-being.

Consider your morning routine: The order in which you do things likely follows a pattern that provides comfort. When this routine is disrupted, it can throw off your entire day. For children, whose prefrontal cortex is still developing, a lack of routine can lead to dysregulation and stress.

Visual routine charts can be particularly beneficial for young children. These charts, featuring words and images, can cover the entire day or focus on challenging parts of the day, like mornings. Placing them in a high-traffic area allows for easy reference throughout the day. It's also crucial to give children ample warning about upcoming transitions, as these can be challenging.

Involving children in creating their routine charts also fosters a sense of belonging and empowerment. This could involve taking photos of them during different daily activities or letting them draw the steps. Another great thing is that when some pushback arises, referring to the chart shifts the focus from parent-directed to chart-directed guidance. For instance, if a child resists brushing their teeth, the chart provides a non-confrontational reminder of what comes next. You are no longer to "blame," as the chart actually says what the steps are, not you. "Oh, I hear you honey, you don't want to brush your teeth. Let's look at our chart to see. Hmm, yeah, the chart does say it's brush-teeth time. Once we finish you can put the checkmark on to show you've completed it! Let's sing our song while we brush to make it extra fun."

Detailed charts for complex tasks, like brushing teeth, help children develop independence by reducing reliance on verbal cues. This approach is especially useful for significant transitions, such as bedtime and nap routines. Consistency is key, even if it means shortening certain steps due to time constraints.

The ultimate goal of parenting is to guide children toward self-sufficiency. Routine charts are a tool toward this end, teaching them to manage and follow structured plans. While they aren't a cure-all for resistance and challenges, they play a significant role in empowering children to feel competent and capable.

In implementing these charts, rewards aren't necessary. Simple visual cues like Velcro check marks or folding tasks away once completed can be effective. Some children might enjoy additional steps like stickers, though this can be more demanding to maintain.

Routine charts and daily rhythms are more than just a parenting tool; they are a means to instill confidence, independence, and competence in children, helping them navigate daily life with greater ease and understanding. The consistency in these tasks that so many kids refuse is eased through the comfort of routine. For kids who really struggle, try implementing a habit-stacking tool to interrupt the usual refusal pattern and shift into a better routine for all. For example: Pair teeth brushing with their favorite song playing! We bring some music in for my child with sensory aversion to teeth brushing and it helps to keep the moment calm and joyful. With this we stack a moment of fun and connection with a task that must be done.

Another helpful language around routines and transitions is *"When, then."*

- "When we brush our teeth, *then* we're ready to play!"

- "When we put our shoes on, *then* we're going to go outside."

"When, then" is so helpful for them to begin understanding the sequence of events. Remember, developmentally they need those reminders.

Below is an example of a typical day in our home with a toddler and a preschooler. We tend to go with the flow, while maintaining a rhythm. I have found this works better than a full, rigid schedule for young children, while still offering the consistency they need to thrive.

We bring as many of these routines outside as possible. That might mean lunch in the backyard, morning play outside, etc.

DAILY RHYTHM

7:30: Wake Up + Morning Cuddles + Snack

8:00–8:45: Morning Play (e.g., Books, Puzzles, Art)

8:45–9:20: Breakfast. Prep Together + Eat

9:20–11:20: Independent Play + Snack Time

11:20–11:55: Lunch. Prep Together + Eat

11:55–1:00: Outside

1:00–2:00: Rest Time (e.g., Books, Quiet Time)

2:00–2:20: Snack Time

2:20–5:00: Afternoon Activity (e.g., Park, Friends, Art, Errands)

5:00–6:00: Dinner. Prep Together + Eat

Begin 6:00, asleep by 7:00
Bed Routine (e.g., Bathtime, Stories, Cuddles, Sleep)

TRANSITIONS

Oh, the dreaded transitions! These are so hard for kids. Heck, change and transitions are hard on adults. Children, like us, experience feelings as they anticipate or react to transitions and show them in their behaviors. Their responses definitely reflect their developmental stage or age, as well as who they are as individuals. Because each child's temperament and prior experiences vary, transitions affect them in different ways. While one child may manage transition smoothly, another may have difficulties.

A great example of this is the child who loves playing outside, yet refuses to go outside. It can feel like it makes zero sense, but it's a big change for them, even though you know they will be happy once they're out there. They get comfortable where they are—the current people they're with, the temperature, the whole environment—it all helps them to know what to expect and what's expected of them in this moment. Then they have to readjust entirely to go onto something new and it's harder than we might think. So, how can we help them?

The first measure of support? Letting them know what's happening in their lives and giving them time to process. I've heard a lot of parents say, "Well, if it's something they don't want to do and I tell them about it ahead of time, then they will have a melt-down right then and start refusing." I hear ya. And yet, it's always better to be respectful and honest about what's coming. Yes, that means when they have a doctor's appointment and we think it best not to mention it until you're already in the car—oh, the panic! We want to give ample time to process changes big and small, and to trust us in the process. For some kids, that might mean a few days before, you take out a library book on going to the doctor and talk about it or role play.

Let's say we're leaving the playground. That's usually a transition where many run into a struggle. The first thing we want to do is give verbal preparation. "In about ten minutes, we'll have to head home, love." Then repeat that in five minutes. And then, when you're getting close to leaving, we like to do an invitation to have one last bit of fun. "We have time for *one* last adventure. What will you choose? The big slide or the swirly slide?" If they have something else in mind, then sure, go for it!

Now, you have decided it's time to go, yes? So be sure you meant that. Of course, there will be a time every now and again where you change your mind and think it's okay to stay, even after you told them it was time to go. So, just be honest about that. You don't have to stick to it like a drill sergeant: "Hey, love, Joey's practice is running a little long, so we can stay for a few extra minutes!" Sure!

Most of the time though, when we say it's time to go, it should be time to go. When we find ourselves repeating and repeating "time to go, time to go," and not actually going, then our words don't exactly mean all that much and they *expect* that they'll be able to stay, since follow-through hasn't been consistent.

Now you've done the last adventure slide and the time has come to leave, so set the limit. "It's time to go."

Offer a choice. "Should we run to the car or hop!? Ready, set, go!" Make it fun and be mindful not to set up the question for a "no."

One of the most helpful tools is a transition song. When we use the same songs for transitions it provides a predictable routine that helps them feel safe and secure in their environment, and safe and secure with *you*. Familiar songs create a sense of comfort for a child. No matter where you are, you always have access to this same familiar tune. Many parents and teachers learn the value of songs for reinforcing routines—like that song you sing every night at bedtime since they were born actually signals to the brain that they are transitioning into sleep mode. The song we sing when we're leaving somewhere, anywhere, is the goodbye song.

This comfortable tune sends a message to the brain to slow down a bit. Put the panic and stress of a transition aside and just know that "hey, when I hear this tune, it means things are changing. My brain recognizes this and I'm okay."

If they're sad that it's transition time, validate those feelings and acknowledge that it's hard to leave somewhere or change from something that you love!

Focus on more "yes." Highlight what you'll be doing when you get home. Will you be making lunch together? Maybe art time? Or use silly invitations to fantasize, "I hear you, love, you want to live at the playground! Oh, man, wouldn't that be crazy? Where would you sleep? Will it get cold? Would you live here alone? What would you eat!? I know you love the playground, but that would be so silly if you lived here, and I would miss you. Yes, we can come back again soon, though!"

*"Goodbye to the
(insert where/what
you are leaving),
I was glad to see you
Goodbye to the (insert here),
I loved to see you
Goodbye to the (insert here),
I will see you again"*

Wave goodbye while singing together

POSITIVE LANGUAGE

A UCLA study found that, on average toddlers hear the word "no" 400 times a day. That's so many times. The chances of anything holding value when heard 400 times a day is pretty nonexistent. When we shift into more positive language and save "no" for the rare times of actual danger, then our "no" holds value and reason, rather than just being a constant, monotonous, angsty word throughout their day.

"Stop it." "No." "Don't do that!"

As a parent, you might find yourself using these words and phrases more often when your child begins to make his own choices. Pause for a moment and consider how the situation might feel if you couldn't use these words. What if, instead of telling your child what he can't do, you instead chose words to tell him what he *can* do, and how he can be successful? While this shift in language might seem small, it actually provides a powerful positive change to the tone and likelihood of your message getting through.

Words like "stop" and "no" don't tell or teach a child much. She's left trying to figure out what she *should be doing,* because there was no clear direction on how to succeed. We can't assume that they know what an appropriate behavior to shift into would look like.

So, maybe you're thinking, "just add what she should stop doing" and this advances the level of confusion. If I say, "No throwing your toys!" She's left to double-process the statement (which is difficult for a young mind!) to figure out what it is I do want her to do versus what I don't want her to do. There are about a thousand alternatives to "not" doing something, but only one course of action when told specifically what's allowed.

The way a human mind understands language is to initially process what comes after the "no" or "stop," sending their mind right to doing that exact same thing, again—by saying, "No throwing your toys!" we know that the part much more likely to be processed first is, "throw your toys!"

Let's try this on your brain.

Don't think about the pink elephant, okay? No thinking about pink elephants.

What are you thinking of? Yep, pink elephants.

We know, based on research from Tina Payne Bryson and Dan Siegel, that anything we give attention to, anything we emphasize in our experiences and interactions, creates new linking connections in the brain. Where attention goes, neurons fire. And where neurons fire, they wire to join together.

In other words, we're making long-lasting positive, effective, and constructive changes to our child's brain by changing the language we use in our parenting.

One easy way to do this is to remind yourself to replace "don't" with "do." Tell your child what she can do! If you saw jumping on the couch, instead of:

"No jumping on the couch!"

Try: "Couches are for sitting. You can jump on the floor!"

It's more likely that your child will make the more appropriate choice when you help them to understand exactly what appropriate options are available. Since they are probably having a ton of fun jumping on that couch, they may not be able to process your words right away, so be sure to physically hold that boundary and help them down to jump on the floor.

As soon as your child begins to follow the instruction or direction, you can immediately reinforce this with a specific observation or comment. So, if you happened to say, "We walk in the house," and your child showed even the slightest sign of slowing down his body from running, you would make eye contact, smile, and say, "Thank you so much for working on your walking feet." You are spending time focusing on what he is doing well to increase those more appropriate behaviors.

Sometimes, it can get frustrating when they don't respond fast enough to our requests and it's tempting to just go in with demands or raise your voice. When that happens, just try to remember that your child is learning language, processing it, and decoding it. She needs time to think about what you said and how she's going to respond. It can take her several seconds—or even minutes—longer than you to process the information. I like to give this a seven count—seven full seconds before I repeat myself. If you remain calm and patiently repeat the statement again, you will see fewer challenging behaviors erupt back at you. Before raising your voice—remember to raise your *words.* Lower your body and get on their level to make sure your words are ones that make sense to them and you're connecting with them. This is much more effective than yelling. Yelling sends the child's brain into fight-or-flight mode and *silences* our message. Then we're left with a scared and heightened child, a disconnection in our relationship, and a child who is unable to listen, or is uninterested in "listening."

Effective alternatives to negative phrases.

Stop hitting!	Gentle hands.
Do not color on the table.	We color on the paper.
No kicking.	Keep your feet to yourself. Our feet are for walking.
Do not touch him/her.	Hands to self.
No standing on your chair.	We sit in the chair.
Do not throw your toys.	Our toys are for playing.
Stop interrupting.	Wait your turn.
Don't jump on the couch.	You can jump on the floor.
I can't stand your screaming.	Please use a quiet voice.
Don't leave your toys on the floor.	Our toys belong on the shelf.
No hitting your brother.	Use gentle and loving hands.
Don't run in the house.	We use walking feet inside.
No!	Tell them exactly what you do want or expect.

GROWTH MINDSET

In the world of education and child development, the concept of a "growth mindset" as compared to a "fixed mindset" has gained significant attention, for good reason. This growth mindset, characterized by a belief in the malleability of intelligence and abilities, has been widely studied and promoted as a powerful tool for fostering resilience, motivation, and a love of learning in children. Basically, it's a big deal!

As we know, Maria Montessori laid the groundwork for an approach deeply rooted in the belief of the limitless potential of each child. In a Montessori home, children are viewed as active, self-driven learners who construct their knowledge through hands-on experiences. This fundamental principle aligns so beautifully with a growth mindset as researched by Carol Dweck about thirty years ago, as she changed education and the raising of little ones forever!

So, what is the growth mindset in practice?

Embracing Challenges

In Montessori, kids get to tackle tough stuff at their own speed. If they're figuring out a tricky math problem or still getting better at using their hands for everyday tasks, they're learning to take on challenges at their own pace without a parent shaming or rushing them. We're intentionally setting them up with a growth mindset that says, "When you hit a hard spot, it's not a roadblock—it's a chance to get even better at something and I trust you to get there!" As children begin to understand that hard work and practice are essential for achieving mastery, we find that kids are more likely to persist in challenging situations.

Embracing Mistakes

We all make mistakes and that's a good thing, because it's a huge indication that we're trying something new or putting effort into what we haven't mastered. Like, I apparently haven't mastered walking with three plates and a travel mug in my hand. Or at least not totally, because I found myself carrying all such things and dropped the travel mug the other day, and guess what happened? My kids saw this and gave me the perfect opportunity to model kindness to myself! Mistakes can be seen as a natural part of the learning process. In this case I said, "Wow, that was a surprise—I didn't expect to drop that! We all make mistakes sometimes, huh? I guess next time I can just carry fewer things at once or use a tray. Would anyone like to help me clean up?"

Note that we aren't just saying, "Whatever, let me leave my messes all over the place because mistakes happen." We intentionally focus on finding solutions to problems together, not shaming for the problem. It's been found that solution-based parent strategies that encourage teamwork and positivity have much more effective results than coercive measures.

One of the most impactful responses to mistakes is the reminder that no "mistake" comes even close to the amount of love we feel for our children or ourselves. "I love you so much more than that broken lamp," or "I love you so much more than any grade you get." This is just as valuable during their big accomplishment moments, too, to emphasize that they are loved for who they are inside, beyond anything they could ever do, good or "bad."

Adults benefit from a growth mindset, too, by the way. The more we can model and truly embrace awesome tools like this, the more likely our kids will soak it in. So, be kind to *you*! As with all things neuroplasticity, it's easier to *build* a child's brain on this than to "retrain" an adult brain, but that doesn't mean it isn't possible. We're all capable of "learning new tricks," as they say. In this case, the trick is a mindset that sees opportunity for growth. It might sound something like shifting a mindset of "I'm a failure" to a more intentional "I'm not great at this yet, but I can prepare for next time to see improvements!"

FIXED MINDSET

Locked on limiting beliefs:

Feels that they are either good at something or not.

Success determines worth.

Not focused on progress or growth.

Focused on outcome over process.

Avoid mistakes, so may choose not to try.

- *"You are so smart!"*
- *"Oh, sweetie, math is just not your subject."*
- *"You're our artist; your sister is the athlete."*
- *"What grade did you get?" (Rather than showing interest in process and thought work)*

GROWTH MINDSET

Pay attention to effort over results:

"Brains can get stronger!"

Use the word "yet," and use it often.

Catch them being persistent.

Be specific with encouragement.

Encourage a healthy attitude toward failure and challenge.

Show them they don't always have to be successful to be okay.

- *"This was a difficult task, but your hard work paid off!"*

- *"Is there another strategy you can try?"*

- *"You have a big task ahead of you. This might take some time."*

- *"Mistakes can help us learn what to do better next time."*

- *"That was a creative way to solve your problem!"*

- *"If you practice, you'll grow to be able to do it on your own."*

3
The Environment

I've always felt that the Montessori environment is best described as an extension of both the adult and the child. An intentional space that both invites the child to expand and flourish, while at the same time, creates limits to keep the child safe within them. The typical home environment is created solely for an adult to thrive in, with little thought to the child. In this chapter, I invite you to get on their level to see the world through their eyes (really, physically get down on their eye level and get curious as it is very helpful!). But also, on a deeper level we want to gain a better understanding of their experience with and in relation to their home.

A PREPARED ENVIRONMENT

A prepared environment is a place in the world created for children to be able to interact, enjoy, and functionally move about, without entirely too much adult intervention. Much goes into the environment, including *you!* The prepared adult creates this environment based on observations, the child's interests, and age-appropriate materials. There are several principles that guide the preparation of the environment: freedom, beauty, and contact with nature.

Why? Well, for one, we think they deserve that! We get to have adult-sized furniture to sit on, adult-height tables to eat at, and can even get a glass of water when we feel thirsty. Why shouldn't children get the same basic respect to move with ease within their environment? It's a beautiful gift to offer them independence and the feeling that they are significant and considered in this family.

And for the second "why," the prepared environment solves problems before they ever even arise, making these early years less of a power struggle and more enjoyable for all. If the goal is a child who feels that they are capable, significant, and that they belong, then setting them up for success is a sure way to help them get there! Consider the environment as a partner in your parenting.

A prepared environment can be created in 400 sq. ft. (37 m2) studio, an RV, a historical mansion, a trailer—I mean anywhere. It's not about the space or the Insta-worthy photo, it's about functionality and following the principles Maria Montessori so clearly and kindly created for us.

So, let's get you a space that solves problems, gives your child the independence they crave, and gives you some of that freedom to sit back and say "yes" instead of "No, I must redirect you!" all day long.

"The first aim of the prepared environment is, as far as it is possible, to render the growing child independent of the adult."

—MARIA MONTESSORI

PROBLEM SOLVING

One of my favorite professors used to have us come up with solutions to an endless list of potential "problems" that could arise in the classroom. The trick of it was, the solutions had to be free of adult intervention, and instead, use the environment as a proactive problem solver. She called this creating a *problem-solving environment.* The first thing I do when I notice a challenge repeatedly arise is see if I can come up with a solution in the environment that either negates the issue entirely or can at least ease it for everyone.

I'll give an example to start. When my son was first born, my toddler daughter sometimes felt left out during his nursing sessions, and a few times got so upset that she tried to go outside without permission. We had a usual lock on the door and up until that point, she couldn't unlock it. Lo and behold, one day she mastered the unlocking, and out she went. Thankfully, I heard the door and ran out after her. The next time I nursed, she did the same thing. And the next time, too. I kept telling her not to do it, and of course, she kept doing it.

By the time my husband got home from work I was so worked up and didn't understand why she was doing this. I tried to connect with her during the nursing sessions, bring a book and invite her to sit with us, let her hold the baby's hand like she wanted to, and thought we were doing so well at including her in this new dynamic.

In stepping back and taking a few deep breaths, I realized a few things that were unclear to me at first.

1. She's still feeling disconnected and this is a cry for help.

2. It must feel very scary to see that mom is so busy with the new baby that she can actually *leave* the house before mom can get to her.

3. It's my job to keep her safe and I need to find a solution.

4. He was nursing on demand in those early days and so I couldn't offer her set routines around this, which made it unpredictable and stressful for her.

Here is what we did:

1. Got locks for the top of all the doors so that she couldn't reach them. We invited her to be part of the process of putting the locks on and told her that now with these door helper locks, she would be safe inside the house.

2. Offered two- to five-minute warnings on when I would be nursing again based on noticing his early hunger cues. We used a little sand timer when we got down to one minute. Just that little heads up went a long way.

3. Created a basket of materials for her to play with that were only available during nursing. I chose materials that she could do with me or alone and would pull it out to be right next to the rocking chair every time.

4. I did also consider the draw to the outdoors, and we added more outdoor time to our routine, as I think she was innately drawn to the fresh air in an attempt to self-regulate.

117

By the next day, all challenges around nursing time were gone. We used the environment to problem-solve and support her.

When evaluating the environment to pinpoint and solve problems, we like to keep these things in mind:

1. **The guide.** It's not just a home; it's a guide. I consider our home to be like a symbolic third parent in our family. The environment acts like a gentle nudge, steering little explorers toward activities that align with their developmental stage and encourage exploration in a safe and appropriate way. Recently, our toddler continued to climb up onto our kitchen island, and so we moved the stools to the garage. Rather than living on edge about his safety and stressing that he'd be drawn to climb up onto the island for something while I was out of the room for a moment, we took the impulse away by removing the stools. Based on developmental age and stage, he couldn't resist this impulse on his own. A few months later, we added the stools back without issue, as he had established appropriate climbing outlets elsewhere. Removing the stools wasn't a punishment, and wasn't framed as such; it was a means to both keep the child safe and respect the developmental need and draw to climb, but in appropriate places.

2. **Child-centric design (where applicable).** Montessori environments are designed with the child's perspective in mind. Furniture, tools, and materials are appropriately sized and arranged to facilitate independent exploration and engagement. This minimizes frustration and encourages a sense of autonomy.

3. **Order and accessibility.** An organized environment reduces confusion and frustration. Everything has a designated place, making it easier for children to locate and return items after use. This promotes a sense of order and helps children develop responsibility for their surroundings.

4. **Limited choices.** Offering a limited selection of activities or materials at a time can prevent overwhelm and decision fatigue. This controlled environment allows children to focus more effectively, promoting deep engagement and concentration.

5. **Safety consideration.** Childproofing measures are in place, and potentially hazardous items are kept out of reach. This minimizes the risk of accidents, allowing children to explore with confidence. You also avoid so many "nos" and redirections by preparing an environment where a child can touch and explore safely.

6. **Clear communication.** Visual cues, labels, and simple instructions are incorporated into the environment to facilitate communication. This empowers children to understand expectations and follow routines independently, reducing the need for constant verbal guidance.

7. **Observation and adaptation.** Regular observation of children's interactions with the environment allows parents and educators to identify potential issues early on. By staying attuned to children's needs and interests, adjustments can be made to better cater to their developmental stage.

SIMPLICITY

If you arrived at work to a cluttered desk with files all in disarray, you'd likely feel stressed right from the start of the day. It would take you longer to complete tasks, fumbling around for the materials you needed, and maybe you'd even give up due to the frustration. Clutter can mess with our heads! First off, stress levels can skyrocket when our space is in chaos. It's like our brains can't catch a break with all that visual noise. Plus, staying focused? Yeah, not so easy in a cluttered space. The guilt trip is real too—that feeling when you know you should tidy up but haven't gotten around to it? Been there. And guess what? Lack of sleep can also join the party if the bedroom's a mess. A tidy room can be a sanctuary for good sleep. A clean, organized space just feels more chill. It's like a breath of fresh air for our nervous systems.

Just as overwhelming environments can impact adults' mental health, it can also affect children. Montessori principles emphasize the importance of an organized and purposeful environment to support a child's natural development and well-being. We hear a lot about preparing the "playroom" for kids, but they are members of the family and feel the energy of the entire home. Now, if you know me in real life, you are probably getting a giggle at this because I'm *not* tidy. By nature, I'm someone who's disorganized, cluttered, and moving along creating things and making messes as I go. When I leave the house in such disarray, the very first thing I notice are more frequent meltdowns and general unease in the kids. So, even though it feels difficult, we've minimized our belongings and keep our space as tidy as we can, without driving ourselves nuts over it. Due to having minimal "things," now it's significantly easier for our kids to help out in the clean-ups and we can all work together as a team.

Where can we start? Well, let's take a look at the toys available to your child. One little human only needs anywhere from four to eight materials available at a time in the first few years of life. The younger they are, the less toys should be out. Having so many items to choose from actually hinders the child's ability to concentrate on one thing, and we find them bouncing from toy to toy, never fully mastering the concepts. Hmm, let's think of the cluttered desk and junk all over the office—this likely isn't your ideal work space, and it isn't your child's either.

No need to toss your toys; donate what doesn't align with your child's needs, and then you can simply put other items into storage and rotate materials in and out. We favor toys that don't operate on batteries, otherwise called "passive toys." Passive toys make your child do the creative work and thinking, rather than a fast and overstimulating reward for little action (e.g., push a button and a toy lights up or sings). Passive toys make active thinkers, and we like that! Your job as the prepared adult is to observe your child. If you see a material (toy) hasn't been getting much action, it's not meeting your child's current needs and can be switched out for something that is. Leave a material out and available to your little one for as long as it's being used.

There's no set time that one must "rotate" a shelf. Keep in mind, by nature, our children *love* consistency and sameness. So instead of having all their toys taken away for a grand reveal of new shelfwork, it'll feel calmer for all to just switch a few materials at a time, when you notice they haven't been paying attention to those lately.

ORDER

A place for everything, and everything in its place.

Children have a sensitive period (more soon) for order from birth through age five, peaking in early toddlerhood. You can see the sensitive period for order through young children's love for routine and repetition (and their sometimes extreme reactions to something being done the "wrong" way or in the "wrong" order). Young children like order in their daily lives, and also in their physical environments, but they definitely need some help to establish that.

INDEPENDENCE

Janet Lansbury created the term "yes space" based on Magda Gerber's teachings on infants and toddlers. This concept grows with our little ones throughout their childhood, though. It's a child-friendly area intentionally set up for them to explore freely. In this space, caregivers aim to say "yes" to most of the child's actions by removing potential hazards and providing age-appropriate activities, allowing for independent exploration while minimizing the need for constant redirection.

Child-sized furniture allows the child to move freely and safely within their space, not relying on adults to help them in and out of furniture. Consider what you can make accessible to the child to increase their opportunities for independence and lessen your need for intervention. Things like snacks, water, washcloths, and age-appropriate cleaning supplies can be prepped and out for the child when they need them—giving them confidence and increasing the likelihood that they'll do these things on their own!

Stools are our best friend in a Montessori lifestyle, making the grown-up world available to a child. The early years may require a kitchen-tower-type stool, giving them extra height and safety to be included in the cooking and prep work. Simple step stools can be placed at the sinks for hand washing and some even fold up nicely to be tucked away, if needed.

There are so many "hacks" to making a Montessori home, and we're going room by room to share some great ideas in the pages to come.

"How does he achieve this independence? He does it by means of a continuous activity. How does he become free? By means of constant effort. We know that development results from activity. The environment must be rich in motives which lend interest to activity and invite the child to conduct his own experiences."

—MARIA MONTESSORI

AESTHETICS

So, imagine a classroom or play area—it's not just a space; it's an experience. Montessori is all about an intentional, cozy, and natural vibe. The value of natural materials like wood, bamboo, metals, glass, and real plants isn't just about looking good. It's because they're real, they're tactile, and they connect kids with the natural world. Wood, being warm and inviting, draws little hands in, encouraging exploration and creativity. We aim for a space that engages the senses, sparking curiosity and creating an environment that's not just visually pleasing, but also mentally and physically stimulating.

The simplicity of neutral tones offers a visual calm that allows the child to focus on what they are drawn to, rather than so many competing stimulants and bright colors. There's an intentional balance of offering rich art experiences and creative design that brings us joy in expressing ourselves versus an overstimulating environment. When evaluating your space, exit the room, take a breath, then walk back in. Notice how you *feel* when you enter. Is it inviting? Is it clearly defined? Is it somewhere you feel calm?

These are all things to consider. One great tip is to get on your child's eye level to see how the space looks to them. If they're crawling, you crawl. Toddling about 2 ft. (.6 m) off the ground? Check that height out too.

Notice how most of the time, children have no visual access to art, mirrors, or other aesthetic delights set to adult height. We love to offer art at the child's level to include them in the experience. This is so valuable for evaluating the feel of the space, but also always take this time to double-check all safety from their eye level. To enhance their visual experience, we added an art wall, including works of our favorite artists, as well as their own art! I love the idea of hanging their work next to famous pieces as an encouragement to their artistic pride and process.

We also have little frames throughout at their level and change the pictures periodically, which brings a lot of excitement! A great tip is to remove the glass entirely (for toddler safety) and tape the picture right in. We use postcards for the art, as they're the perfect size and a pack comes with so many lovely works of art.

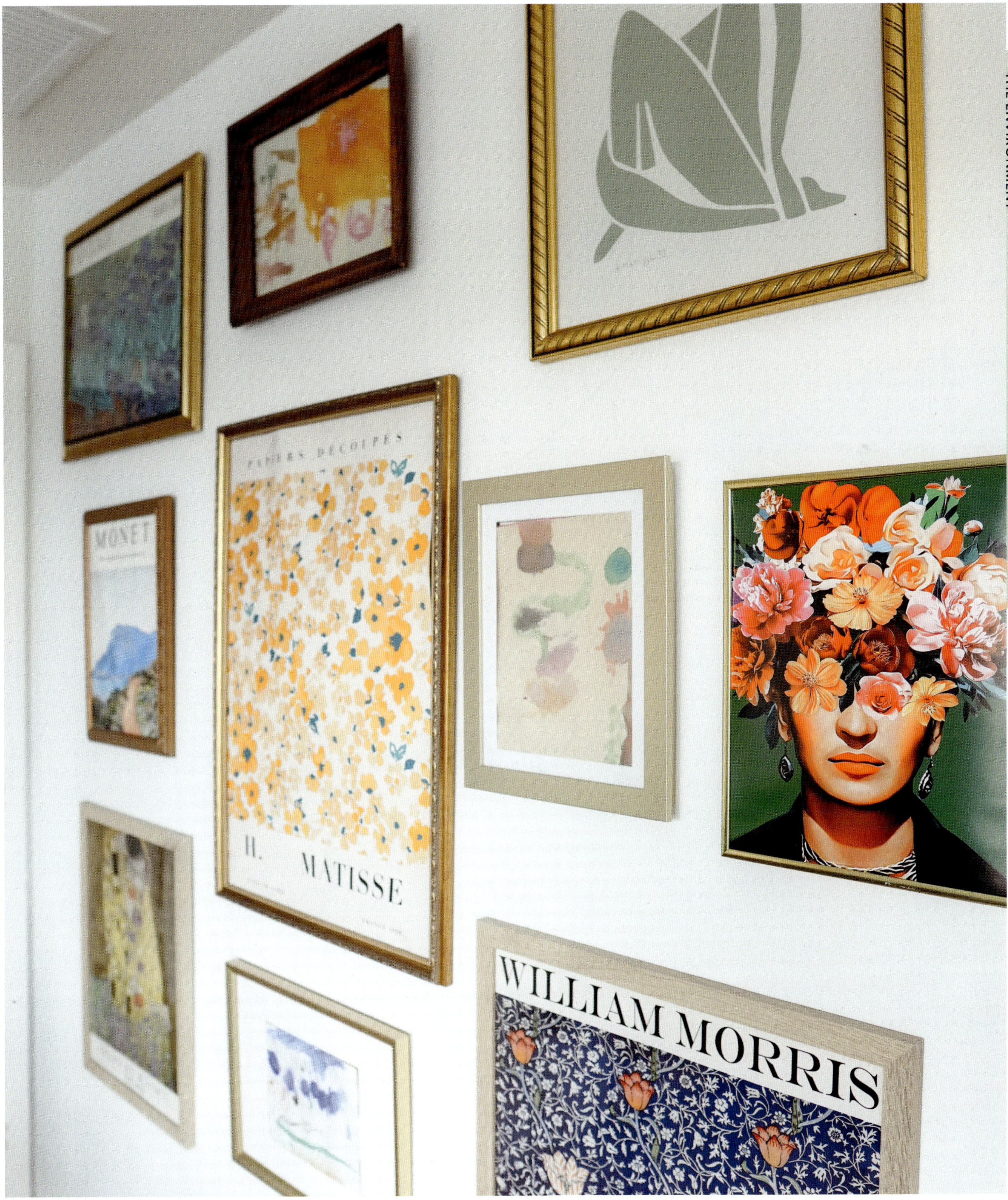
MONET
PAPIERS DÉCOUPÉS
H. MATISSE
WILLIAM MORRIS

MAKE, THRIFT, SCAVENGE

One of the biggest barriers to a Montessori lifestyle is the false belief that it's not affordable. When my daughter was little, we were living on just my husband's teaching salary in a tiny city apartment. The thought of doing Montessori on a budget seemed like a stretch, especially with all those fancy Montessori "toys" seen online. But guess what? We moved around a lot in those early years—from a one-bedroom to staying with in-laws, and a few rentals in between. Each place had its challenges, but we made it work, because Montessori isn't about having the perfect space or stuff; it's about getting creative with what you've got or can find at the right price.

This thrifted IKEA pieces in all three of these pictures, for instance, has been many things over the years for us! None of them are its intended use, but it's been perfect to adapt for different stages and ages.

127

Using what you have or hunting for second-hand items is also a great way to be kind to the planet and model our role as environmental stewards, making choices that help rather than harm our environment. Those magical, crazy early years zip by fast, and a lot of the stuff you need can be found at thrift stores, passed on by families who've moved to the next stage already. The cycle of donating and thrifting keeps these items out of landfills and in use for years. It's such an impactful part of Montessori—finding preloved stuff, saving up for a few quality sourced items, and making a positive impact on the environment.

Check out local thrift stores, "Buy Nothing" groups, Facebook Marketplace, Mercari, OfferUp, local parenting groups, or even a dedicated children's thrift store, if you can find one. And don't forget to ask around—friends or family with older kids often have hand-me-downs they're happy to pass on. My kids now actually prefer hand-me-downs, knowing they come already full of love and joy from other kids.

And remember, you don't need every single Montessori material you see online. There are heaps of creative ways to teach the same concepts with everyday items or stuff from nature. Plus, if your child goes to a Montessori school, it's better not to duplicate classroom materials at home. But hey, if you find a great deal on some materials or want to invest in certain things, go for it! Just know you don't have to break the bank to give your child an enriching Montessori experience. Maria Montessori herself was all about DIY, and a lot of what's used in classrooms can be replicated at home in simpler, budget-friendly ways.

Take the Montessori ball drop, for example. You might see it pop up in online searches as a must-have. Sure, it's a great tool for developing skills in little ones, but guess what? You can mimic it with a shoebox and any old ball. Seriously, it's that simple. Just take a look at that two-minute DIY to the right!

The classic Montessori wardrobe that we all love can also be DIYed easily, as seen on the previous page, or search around like we did on Facebook Marketplace for "dress up wardrobe" to find something similar with a much lower price tag than something advertised as a "Montessori Children's Wardrobe."

Also, keep in mind that many of the Montessori social media accounts are either gifted or paid to post materials, furniture, or toys for a Montessori home, and this is their job! Influencing you to feel you need these things is why they are paid to do it. Sharing what we use and like in our home now is an aspect of my own "job" too and I'm very grateful for the opportunity to work with the brands I've come to know and feel aligned with. Just be sure you're following accounts who are authentic and honest about these things. I'd love to invite you to scroll and cleanse your feed of any account that brings up feelings of guilt or feeling "less than" in any way, not just materialistically, as you want to surround yourself with inspiration and goodness in all aspects of life—even social media!

And remember, *you* are the most important aspect of your child's upbringing and environment. They'll cherish your love and presence far more than anything you ever buy for them. They won't remember if they had the fancy toy, but they'll remember how you made them feel. You are enough—everything else is just sprinkles on top.

MONTESSORI SPACES

We're going room by room to chat about what makes a space Montessori, and what the value is for your child. Let's start right at the front door!

Entryway

Accessibility, independence, and transition support are the goals of an entryway. In this space, the child is able to move through their getting-ready or coming-home transition with thoughtful ease.

From the weather chart, supporting them to figure out what outerwear clothing is best, to the little stool to sit in while putting on their shoes, to the child-height hooks or pole, everything has an intention behind it. Here starts the concept of a place for everything and everything in its place, as we all know half the time they can't get shoes on simply because they can't find them! When shoes and jackets have a specific home, that issue stops being a barrier for them. Consider shoes and jackets that the child can put on independently to boost that confidence, too!

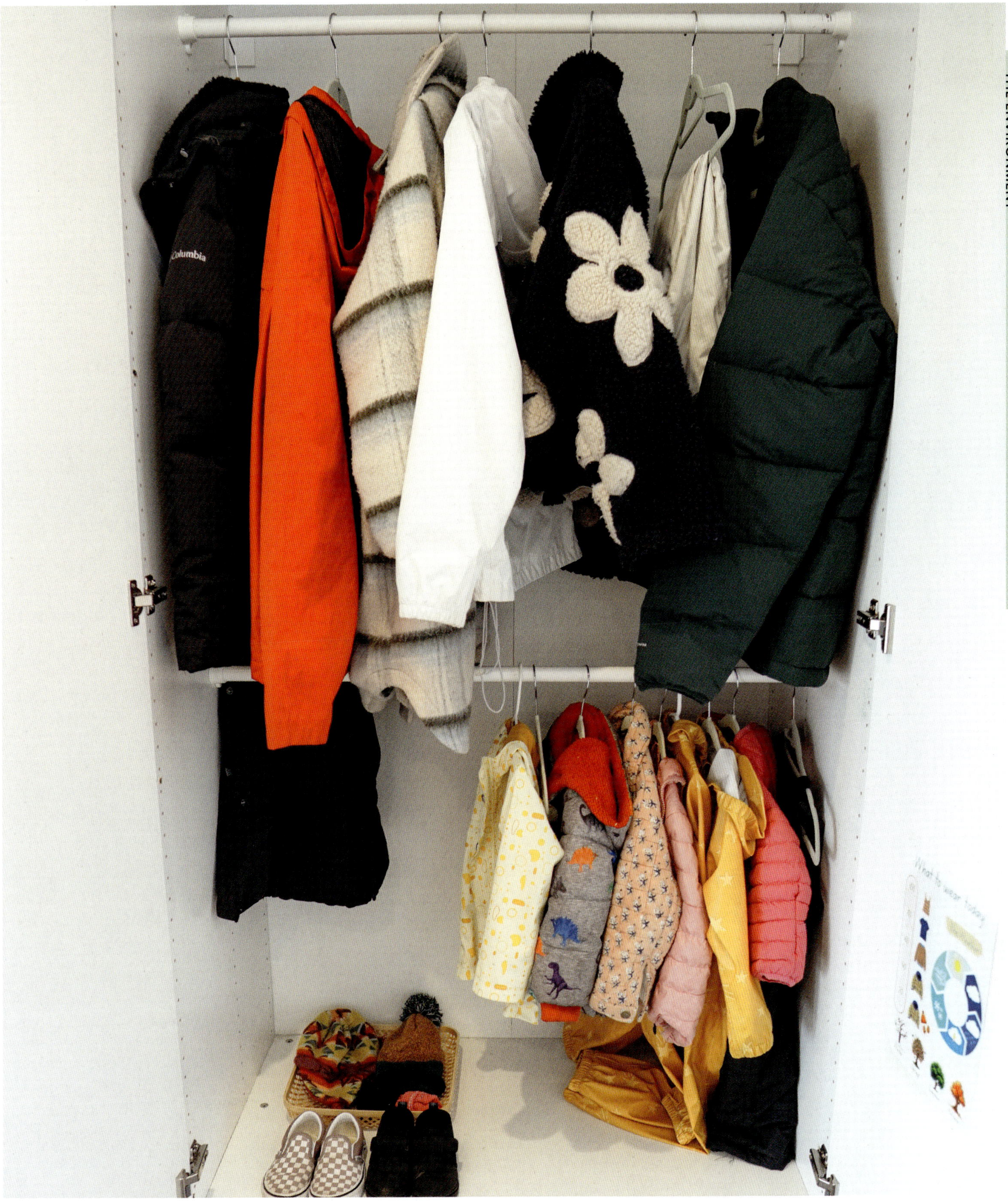
Columbia
What to wear today

Kitchen

The functional kids' kitchen remodel is Montessori-famous these days. And guess what, while it is wonderful if it works in your home layout, it isn't *needed*. Don't get me wrong—we had one, loved it, used it, and then realized with the space we had available, it just wasn't working for us. Instead, we made aspects of our kitchen accessible to the children and that has worked out great. If you are thinking the functional child-sized kitchen would work better in your space or for your child, then definitely go for it! It's all about exploring what's going to work for the whole family. The main aspects of the functional kitchen is a real water source, either by a plug-in or battery-operated faucet hack or water dispenser with spigot. And also, counter space to prepare food, which offers them endless opportunities in developing practical life, motor skills, and much more.

To make the household kitchen more inclusive to your children, consider changing up the organization to put their kitchenware in a lower cabinet/drawer, placing step stools/kitchen tower strategically to invite them to work at counter height, and of course, as always, put child safety measures in place to clearly define what *is* available to the child and what isn't.

By inviting kids into the kitchen, we give them a real place in our little community. There are few confidence boosts like the pride they feel making real food for themselves and those they love! Don't be surprised if you notice your child taste testing and getting more excited about trying new foods once you begin cooking together. Research shows that children are more likely to eat a variety of foods when they are included in the cooking process! Things become more social, lighthearted, and fun when they're connecting with parents in a pressure-free environment where they might pop some new flavors in their mouths. This is a great tool in creating a safe, comfortable environment for a child who leans on the "picky" side or is working through some sensory processing difficulties with food.

As it's been said, the kitchen is the heart of the home, and in a Montessori childhood, it's usually very true. I always tell parents that if you do nothing else, but want to incorporate some aspects of that Montessori goodness in your family, bring your child into the kitchen. Practice patience for you, build their confidence, boost those feelings of significance, and bring more connection to your daily lives, simply by chopping some veggies together.

Part of inviting kids in the kitchen is being sure that the tools they are using are developmentally appropriate and safe. Here are some of our favorite kitchen tools that fit in those little hands. Be sure to stay close and model proper use of all tools.

Now, where to eat that delicious food? Is the best place a highchair, weaning table, or an adjustable dining chair at the family table? You decide! We're big fans of doing what works for your family and offering what we can in terms of giving children the independence they deserve to navigate mealtimes with ease.

Highchair

Safety is the biggest pro for a highchair. You know you can buckle them in, set the tray, and they're contained there for mealtime. While containers may be a contrast to Montessori, in theory, I know in practicality, I'm not the only one who uses them!

Why we like it:
- Perfect height to be seated alongside the family during mealtimes. It's nice to have a moment daily with the whole family sitting together and connecting (toddler included!)

- Supports the toddler in proper position for eating and swallowing for safety (sitting upright with feet flat on a footrest)

- Helps to set defined routines and mealtime expectations

Also keep in mind:
- We honor the child's pleas to get up if they don't want to be in the highchair and are done eating

- Consider the age of the child and explore options to move out of highchair into toddlerhood

How we use it:
- We had a highchair only for a few months with my first child, as space didn't permit for one. We moved her into a booster at the table with us at age one and then found an adjustable Tripp Trapp chair on Facebook Marketplace after some time.

- For the second child, we used a highchair from six months to age two for family mealtimes. Now, he sits at the table with us in the Tripp Trapp chair. For lunch and snack time, our kids typically sit at their child-sized table and chairs together, which they very much enjoy, too!

Weaning Table

The weaning table lends opportunity to the idea that children are capable of independently managing their mealtime and intuitive eating. It's designed for them to come to it and sit in the chair on their own, fostering independence and helping them recognize their hunger cues. Consistency in routine and clear boundaries enhance this setup, enabling the child to thrive. With a table and chairs sized just right, children take immense pride in their dining space, engaging in practical life skills. They learn to set and clear the table, a process that includes arranging placemats, silverware, plates, and cups, and sitting properly with their feet on the ground.

This routine offers valuable lessons in practical life skills, as well as grace and courtesy. It boosts the child's confidence, making them feel trusted and capable. Despite inevitable spills and a learning curve that tests patience, the joy and pride in a child's face are rewarding. For them, what may seem mundane to us is a magical opportunity to feel competent, confident, and a contributing member of the household, mirroring the activities of adults.

Adjustable Chair at Table

The adjustable chair, along with its various adaptations, offers a versatile solution for growing with a child from infancy, featuring attachments and adjustments for every age onward. Though the initial cost of these chairs are often high, its durability and longevity justify the investment if it's within the budget. I found a thrifted one as shown with my son sitting in it to the right, used by a mother for fifteen years and still in near perfect condition, which I'd say speaks to its lasting value. These chairs make it possible for the child to sit right at the table with everyone, through every stage. With the seat and footrests being adjustable, it creates a personalized and safe fit as the child grows. As shown, to the right, my daughter sits in a white IKEA version that isn't adjustable, but does function well for her age and the cost was in budget. Remember the perfect "must-have" material is one that fits a child's needs, a family budget, and space in your home!

Mealtime Tools

Child-sized everything continues with small silverware to fit and support those fine motor skills and the infamous open cup. Offering the child glass cups might seem crazy, but parents are often surprised by how well this goes. Why might this be? Kids feel pride in the trust we give them. When we say, "This is a fragile cup that we take great care of. It's glass, just like I use," and model the gentle intention of use with your own glass, from the way you take a sip to the careful placement back onto the table, they'll be watching you and prepared to mirror your movements. It's much more about what you do/model than what you say. Upon misuse of any material, we offer help. That might look like a child pouring water out or maybe they're about to or already have tossed the cup. A boundary there sounds like, "It looks like you are done drinking out of your cup. Cups are only for drinking. I'll put it away safely and we can try again later."

By introducing children to open cups rather than relying solely on sippy cups or bottles, we encourage self-sufficiency in daily activities. The use of open cups also provides a sensory-rich experience, allowing children to directly engage with the temperature, texture, and taste of the liquid, while also, very importantly, contributing to comprehensive sensory development and oral motor skills. This is another one of those patience builders from parents as little ones practice these skills! P.S., though—if you need to use a sippy cup for your own sanity sometimes, go ahead, my friend. This is a balance.

Family Meals

When it comes to family mealtimes, there's more to them than just eating together. I try to think of them like a special little date with the family, and treat it with that type of respect. No devices at the table, everyone's voices are heard, and genuine interest is reciprocated. It's the perfect time to authentically fill the parent–child connection cup.

Research tells us that these regular sit-downs are super important for kids' growth in all sorts of ways. Think of it as a daily mini-classroom where your kids organically pick up new words, get a taste of family and cultural traditions, and even learn to munch on healthier food, in a pressure-free environment. It's

not just about good manners; it's about chatting, sharing stories, and learning to listen. Kids who have the opportunity for family meals at least four times a week often end up with better self-esteem, tend to do well in school, and are generally more resilient. So, those family dinners are actually a big deal, helping kids feel connected and giving them a solid start in life.

Sitting down together for dinner can even be a dual opportunity for family meetings, which open up the floor for beautiful conversations, real-life problem-solving of situations that impact the family, and learning more about your kids. Family meetings are like team huddles for your household where everyone gets a say. It doesn't have to be done at mealtime, but some like to pair these meetings alongside a fun pizza dinner or have a game night afterward.

You can hold them once a week or whenever suits your family. However frequent, though, it's meant to be an important spot on the calendar. Here's the concept:

- **Everyone Joins In:** From the littlest to the oldest, everyone gets an opportunity to speak up. It's a valuable way to make sure everyone feels heard.

- **Chat About Anything and Everything:** You could be planning a fun outing, solving a little squabble, or figuring out who does what chore. It's all about teamwork.

- **Learning Big Skills in a Comfy Setting:** These chats are great for kids to learn how to express themselves, understand others, and solve problems together.

- **Setting the Scene for Success:** Use these meetings to lay down some family ground rules or celebrate the wins, big or small. As parents, you get to show how to have respectful conversations, even when you disagree.

This ritual of gathering, sharing, and connecting over meals plays a pivotal role in nurturing a child's emotional, social, and cognitive growth, laying a strong foundation for their overall well-being.

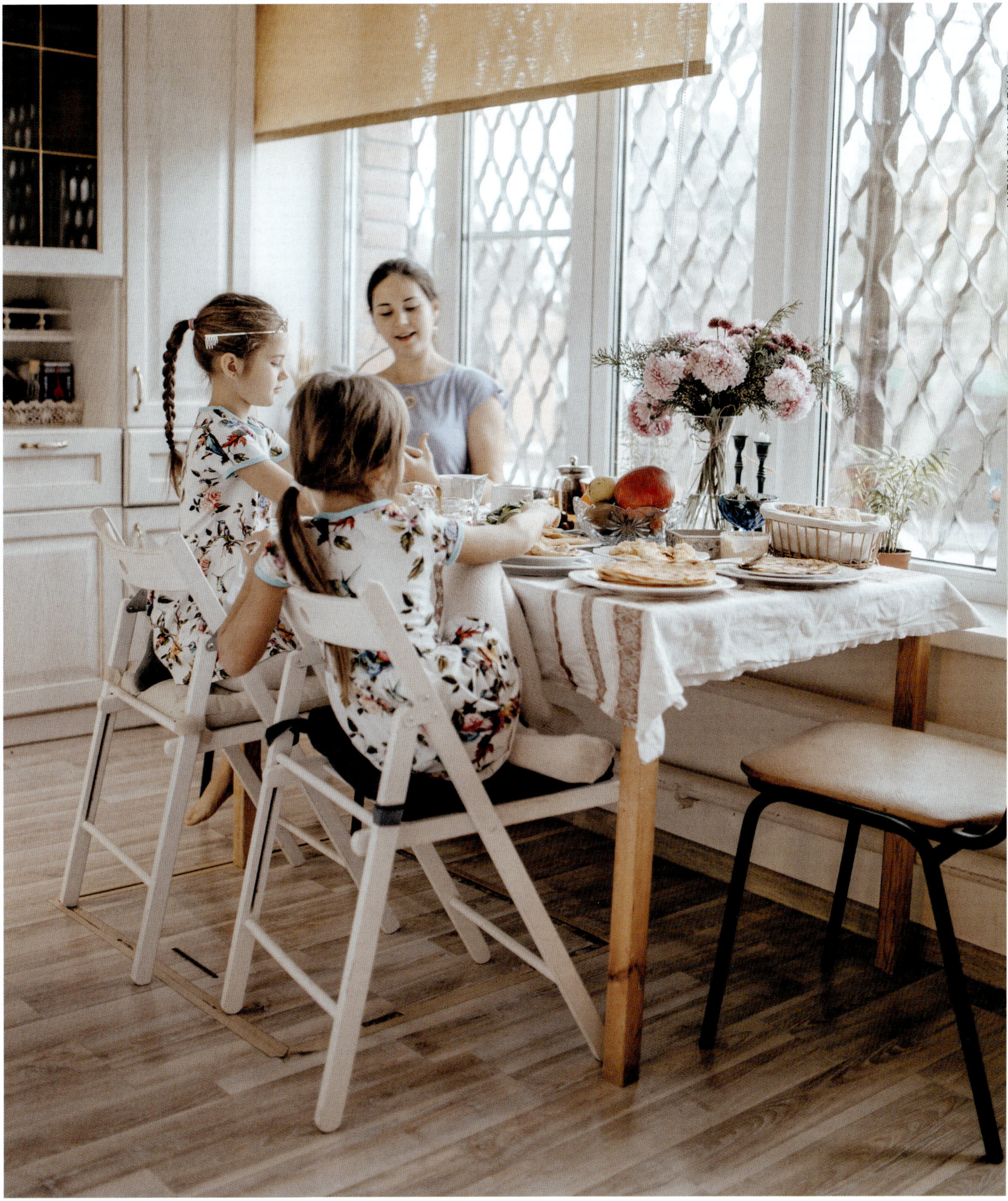

Bedroom

The best-known aspect of the Montessori bedroom is the floor bed. Of course, Maria Montessori didn't "create" the concept of sleeping on a mattress on the floor. This is common practice for many cultures and parts of the world!

What makes it "Montessori" then? The idea is all about giving kids some independence and freedom right from the start. From the time a child would typically go to a crib, we would instead introduce a floor bed. With a floor bed, little ones can crawl on and off when they wake, fostering a sense of autonomy. Plus, it's a safety win—because this book focuses on toddlers and up, we all know those crib-climbing acrobatics to get out of the crib can get intense! The floor bed instead promotes a cozy, calm vibe and encourages a child's natural exploration and movement. Most worries about a floor bed are that the child will constantly get out of bed in the night, and yet, by supporting the child in fostering healthy developmentally appropriate sleep habits, that becomes a nonissue.

When preparing a Montessori bedroom, we have to consider that the child must be completely safe when unsupervised if they do happen to do some nighttime or early morning exploring. This means all outlets are covered, plugs are hidden/secured, and nothing is hanging that can be pulled down or become a safety hazard like the string of your blinds. Remove risky climbing opportunities and be sure that any furniture is completely anchored to the wall. This is exactly when that "yes" space comes into play in a serious way! Magda Gerber explained that you want the space to be so safe that, if by some horrible accident, you got locked out of your house for some amount of time, they would be perfectly safe until you were able to get inside. Of course, that's an extreme example that we take every precaution to avoid, but it gives clarity on how we want to evaluate the room.

The debate on if toys should be in a bedroom is always present, but keep a few things in mind. The bedroom should be a calm, peaceful retreat, and if that means adding a few toys to the space for your child to play with in the morning, then go for it. Consider that it's best to avoid overstimulating toys or ones that they wouldn't be able to resist getting up to play with. We keep books, one or two puzzles, and stuffies in the kids' rooms, which seems to be a nice balance for them. If you observe that the child is more focused on playing than sleeping, it would be best to explore if some materials would be better suited in a room meant for play/work.

"One of the greatest helps that could be given to the psychological development of a child would be to give him a bed suited to his needs."

—MARIA MONTESSORI

Here we find the wardrobe! Kids (just like adults!) love having a say in what they wear and using clothes as a way of expressing themselves. From the earliest days of holding up options for the baby to choose which shirt suits them best, to toddling into grabbing their outfit choice off the hanger, your child may surprise you in just how opinionated they are with their attire. They know what colors they're most drawn to, what materials feel best, and what's comfiest and the best fit. It might save a few minutes to pick clothes out for the child ourselves, but what do we risk in terms of them expressing themselves and feeling confident in the way they present themselves to the world if we always take over that awesome opportunity for them?

The wardrobe gets a lot of hype, and we love the child-sized ones, yet it can be much simpler. Just hanging a lower tension rod in the closet to hang clothes on is a very simple solution! Using little baskets on the floor works too. Keep in mind that we want to keep the wardrobe minimal, with just a few options available to avoid feelings of overwhelm, as this can quickly turn a child from excited to unable to complete the task of choosing their clothes and getting dressed with decision paralysis.

For maximum autonomy, we offer clothes appropriate for their stage of development. For example, small buttons are likely too difficult for a toddler's fine motor skills, or maybe jeans would hinder potty learning with the difficulty of getting them on and off. These are just things to be conscious of, because when they can choose their own clothes and work hard to put them on (even if they're only able to do a tiny bit at a given age), we see so much joy! When was the last time you noticed and smiled about your ability to put socks on alone? Probably not since you were little and an adult gave you the time to do it yourself!

For kids still learning how to dress independently, focus on stopping your help at the point where they can continue on without you. Early on, this looks like helping them get their feet into the pants, but leaving them around the ankle and inviting them to pull them on fully. Socks—just get onto the toe area so they can pull the sock over the heel. And of course, the oh-so-fabulous Montessori coat flip. (A quick search online will show you videos that explain this much better than words can!)

A bedroom is such a special place—one that the child feels is their own. We want them to feel that it's an expression of self, while balancing that calm energy, conducive for rest. A home looks different for everyone, and however your safe sleeping arrangements work out for you is what's perfect for your family! For those who share a sleeping space, consider still offering a child something that's just for them. That might be one drawer that's truly their own, or a shoe box where they can keep a few of their special possessions to themselves without worrying that a sibling will take it. It's such a simple way to show the child that we honor their belongings, plus respecting those things even decreases sibling rivalry challenges. When you think about it, a child technically owns nothing more than their name. When a child can feel secure in having a few of those just-for-me items, we understand why things ease up in the sharing department.

Whether it's the clothes they wear or the red truck they tuck into their personal drawer, we're finding opportunities to tell our child through every action that we love them, we respect them, and we support them for exactly who they are.

142

"Children always reveal to us the most vital need of their development, saying: 'Help me to do it alone!'"

—MARIA MONTESSORI

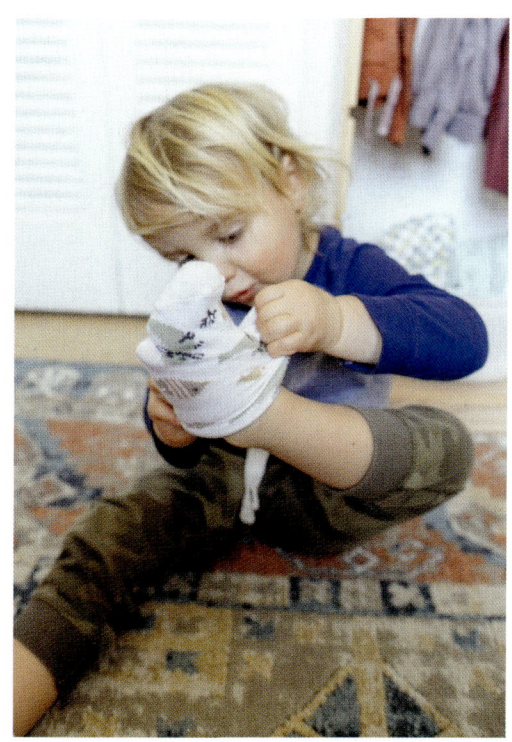

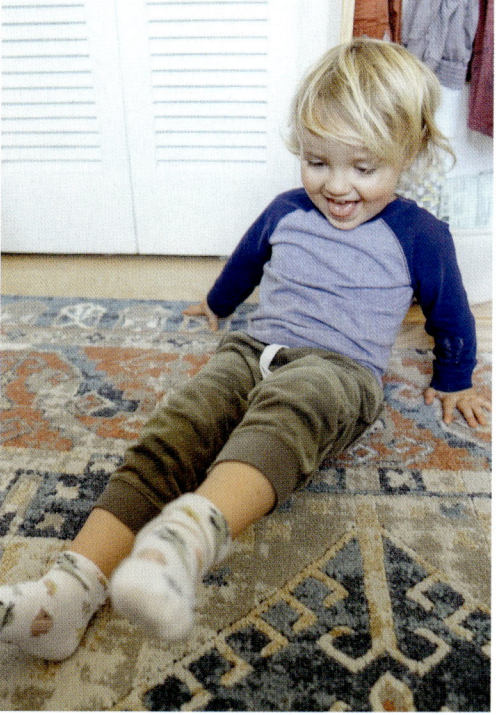

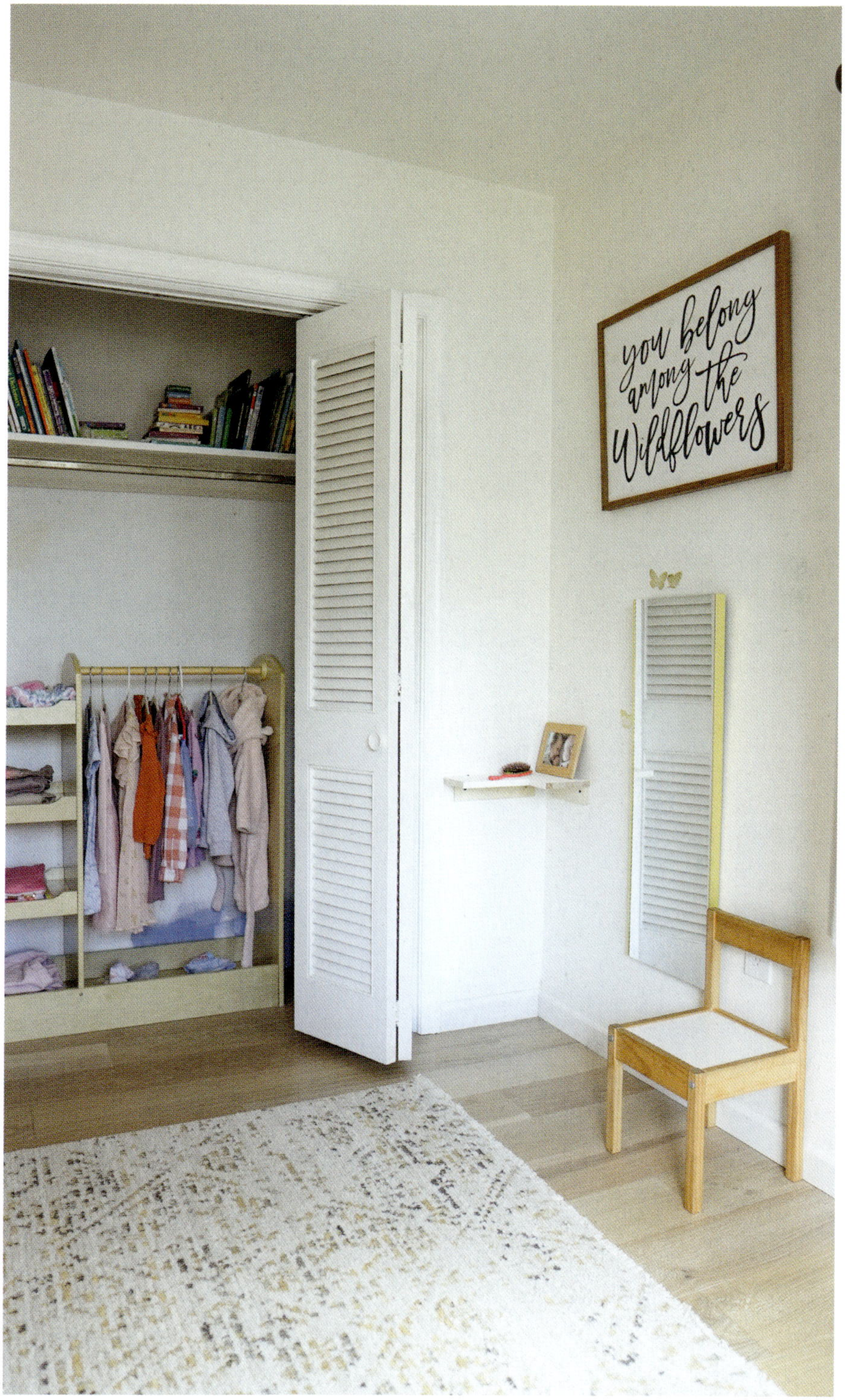
you belong
among the
Wildflowers

Bathroom

Depending on space, we can keep it super simple or elaborate on the child's selfcare opportunities in the bathroom. As I'm sure you've started to gather, we're just aiming to give as many chances for independence as we can in the environment. Due to space, we keep it simple with a step stool in our bathroom and selfcare materials accessible/in reach to the children. This is the perfect place to work on practical life skills! Here are a few other ideas for the space.

We want to set our little ones up for success when it comes to toilet learning, and an environment intentionally created with independence in mind is a huge asset!

When creating an intentional potty-learning environment, we want to be proactive about what is available and easily accessible to both the parent and child. Creating a supply bin in the area makes the potty-learning process much less stressful for everyone involved. We like to keep handy a rag and nontoxic cleaning spray (so that the child can help clean up if they did not make it to the toilet in time), underwear and fresh clothes, a book, and some wipes. By creating a bin like this, we make life easier in the moment, yes, but we also minimize the child's shame and the parent's frustration. By making accommodations and preparing for such things, it shows that this is just a normal part of potty learning and we can simply clean up and change clothes. Children and floors are washable. Broken spirits are much harder to fix, so be gentle in this potty-learning process. For more information on Montessori potty learning, I recommend the book, *Toilet Awareness: Using Montessori Philosophy to Create a Potty Learning Routine* by Sarah Moudry.

Play Space

The key is to create an environment that encourages independence, exploration, and a love for learning. Flexibility is crucial, as the play space is ever-evolving to meet the changing needs and interests of the kids as they grow. And most important is functionality—for the parents and the kids. We often see play spaces tucked away in a different room, a "playroom"—yet, with a lot of feedback from parents, we know that kids are likely to play more if the opportunity is in the main living spaces. Why is this? Well, they want the family to be all together! And it's right there, catching their interest and inviting them in. In the early years especially (hello toddlers), feelings of connection are very linked to physical proximity. When the child feels their adult is close by, they have a sense of calm and freedom to concentrate on the work/play.

Remember independence blooms only from a confident attachment base, so if you're troubleshooting why the child is struggling to play on their own, consider that maybe the play space can be changed to a central location like the living room. While I know play spaces can feel overwhelming or messy, and that's why people tuck them into a separate room, the idea we want to embrace is that the Montessori-aligned play space we're creating is *not* overwhelming and can even bring a pleasant aesthetic that's palatable to adults and ideal for children, too!

Research finds that parents are more likely to engage in connection-based play with their child if the space is of a neutral/natural feel— not full of overstimulating colors, sounds, lights, etc. Research also finds that children are better able to hold concentration and focus on the materials that interest them when the environment isn't overstimulating. This is one of the many Montessori lifestyle concepts that find a lovely overlap in benefits to parents and children.

If you're worried about space, keep in mind that they don't need so very much.

What are we looking for in a prepared environment that fosters independent play, organic learning, and tons of fun?

Open Shelving

This invites kids into the space to see what interests them, rather than having materials in bins/cabinets/hidden away. By having defined space on the shelves, with individual work on trays when applicable, we help the child in choosing what they want with less visual distraction, as well as helping them know where to put things away. The child is able to pick up a tray, as modeled by the adult, and bring it to the floor or table where they choose to work. When finished, materials are put back onto the tray all together, then placed on that spot on the shelf. Having appropriate art materials available to the child also adds a lot of fun!

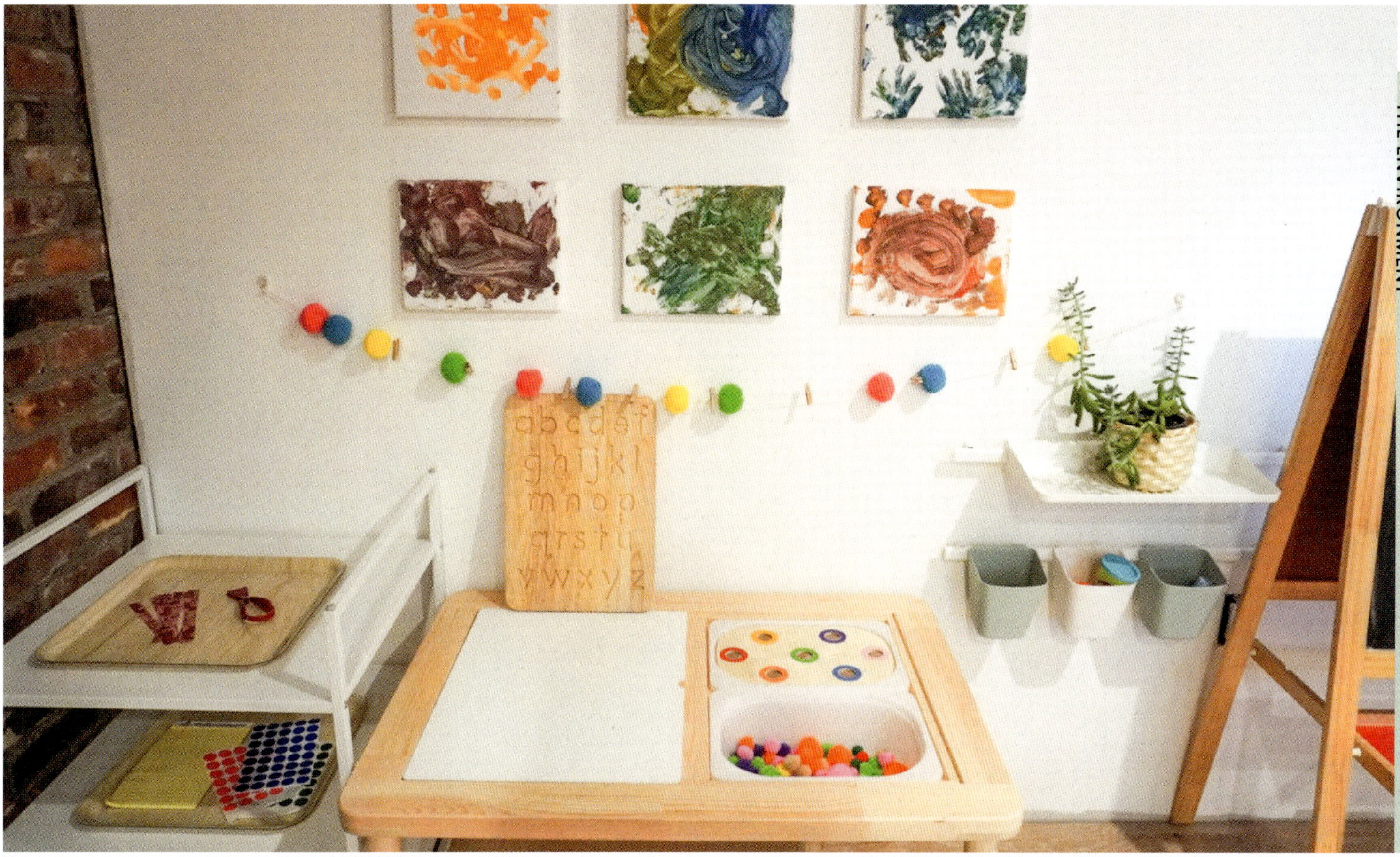
abcdef
ghijkl
mnop
qrstu
vwxyz

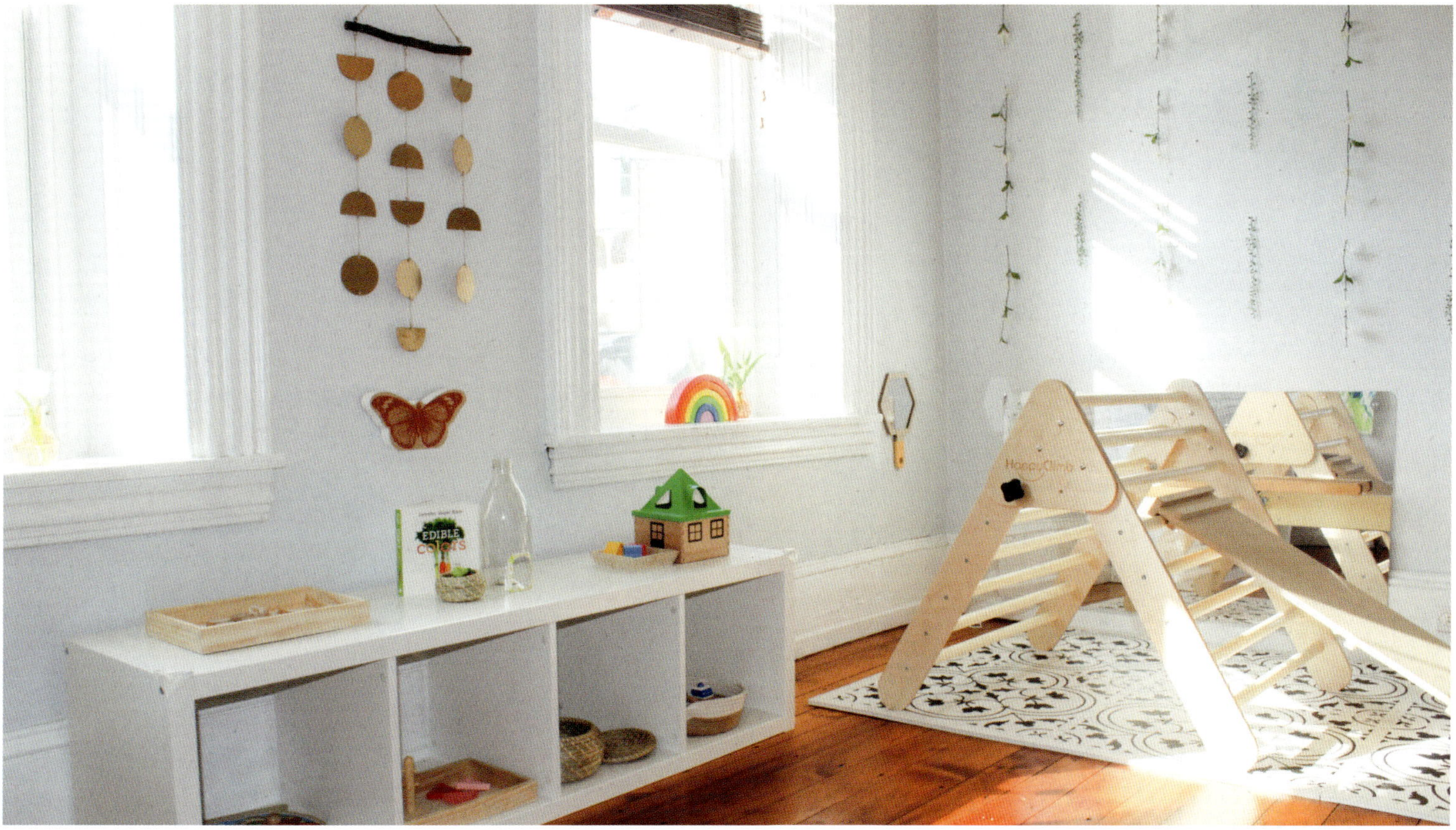
EDIBLE

Materials Available

While Dr. Montessori observed this herself, new research confirms that when it comes to toys, less might be more. A study from the University of Toledo in the United States looked at toddlers aged eighteen to thirty months during playtime. Some kids had sixteen toys to choose from, while others had just four. The ones with fewer toys were way more into their play. The study found that having a ton of toys around actually lowered the quality of toddlers' engagement. The researchers suggested that having fewer toys could help kids focus better, get more creative with their play, and overall, support their development in a healthier way. So, it turns out that simplicity might be the key to keeping playtime focused and fun for the little ones! We find four to eight materials on the shelf at any given time just right.

- Child-sized furniture/table and chair. This pairs as their meal table

- Art hung at the child's level

- Neutral colors; add personal touches that bring joy

- Natural light, if possible

- Calm/peace area for regulation

- Live plants to care for

- Books on display, uncluttered, covers facing outward. Children are less likely to find interest in a book if they are only seeing the spine of the book. The covers draw them in and invite reading time!

- Mirror: Promotes self-recognition and sensory exploration, aiding in the development of identity and body awareness. Additionally, mirrors facilitate social interaction, language development, and cognitive stimulation, offering a holistic developmental experience for young children.

- Rhythm/routine chart

- Clean-up tools accessible to the child to care for their space

Make the space work for your family, create an environment that fits into the home aesthetic and don't be afraid of pops of color. There's a difference between beauty and overstimulation, and you're the judge of that in your home. While simplicity has many benefits, you want to love this space and you know what's right for your family!

Outdoors

Yep, we prepare outdoors, too. I'll spare you from repeating why because it's for all the same benefits!

NATURE

Time spent outside has a significantly positive impact on the brain development of young children. When we step outside various senses are immediately stimulated, cognitive functions are enhanced, and overall well-being is boosted. Simple, yet magical, activities such as exploring nature, playing in the fresh air, and moving those bodies outdoors contribute to improved attention, creativity, emotional regulation, and the development of essential motor skills. The multisensory experiences in nature help shape neural connections, fostering healthy and robust brain development in young children—also, kids sleep better after a day outside and we can all agree that's amazing. Research at the University of Illinois reported that kindergarteners who spent time during the school day in outdoor green spaces were better able to regulate themselves—that is, "better able to attend to social cues, not act on impulse, [and] delay gratification."

I've always loved the reminder that if the kids are bouncing off the walls, remove the walls. Get outside! In that first breath of fresh air, we see the impact on our child's and our own nervous systems. The benefits continue on as the minutes outside go by. Studies show that spending time outside reduces cortisol, the body's stress hormone. It can decrease muscle tension and regulate heart rate, which has a calming effect on the nervous system. It also helps boost the brain's feel-good chemicals like endorphins, dopamine, and serotonin. While the research on this is so vast, I wonder if we need it all. Do we need to be *told* exactly how it impacts us? Instead, what if we stepped outside and truly *felt* how the breeze helps us to take a deep, healing breath in, how the sounds soothe us, and how the view captivates us? By bringing intention to the way we feel in our own bodies, and inviting our kids to notice that too, we step into a mindfulness that has all but escaped us in our hustle and bustle culture. We have access to one of the most powerful regulatory tools in the universe right out that front door, and it's a profound gift we give to our children by teaching them that.

"Let the children be free; encourage them; let them run outside when it is raining; let them remove their shoes when they find a puddle of water; and, when the grass of the meadows is damp with dew, let them run on it and trample it with their bare feet; let them rest peacefully when a tree invites them to sleep beneath its shade; let them shout and laugh when the sun wakes them in the morning as it wakes every living creature that divides its day between waking and sleeping."

—MARIA MONTESSORI

I know it seems so simple, yet I just don't see enough reminders for us parents to utilize the innate draw our bodies feel to the outdoors. From the earliest days of life, when that baby cries and cries, trying to adjust to their body and the whole world around them, notice the calm they settle into upon that first change of air from indoors to outdoors. When my daughter was brand new, we lived in that tiny city space and I'd sit out on the back step for as many hours a day as I could, because it was the only place my sweet, highly sensitive baby girl was calm. In my arms, bundled, with one tiny tree as nature's perfect mobile. Now, at age five when she's having a tough time regulating emotions, she always, always says, "I just need to go outside, mama." And so we do.

We aim for four to six hours a day outdoors, seriously! Living in the northeast, the weather doesn't always cooperate, but we try our best. In the coldest months, we manage between one and two hours broken up throughout the day. While the saying, "There's no such thing as bad weather, just bad attire" gets the point across, it has a blind spot when it comes to being inclusive. Appropriate outdoor clothing can be expensive, cleaning dirty outdoor clothes is time consuming, and space in nature can also be sparse depending on where you live. I'm lookin' at you, icy city sidewalks! Just know that wherever you are and whatever outdoor time you can safely manage, is enough. We're all just trying our best and you're doing great.

"When children come into contact with nature, they reveal their strength."

—MARIA MONTESSORI

You'll likely notice that when your child is in nature, their attention span increases rather dramatically. Whether they are running to chase a butterfly, examining the bark of a tree, digging in the dirt, or staring at the sky, these are all concentration-building moments. It would be no surprise to see that the child can dig in dirt for twenty minutes, but only sit at a desk for two. Notice that, get curious about it, and consider where the child truly thrives. Because, as Dr. Montessori said, "There is no description, no image in any book that is capable of replacing the sight of real trees, and all the life to be found around them, in a real forest. Something emanates from those trees which speaks to the soul, something no book, no museum is capable of giving." All of the sensory goodness we try so hard to replicate and bring into a child's home environment is there waiting for them in the trees, the dirt, the rocks, the ocean, rivers, sand, and snow. Nature is the most glorious "sensory bin," and the cool thing is, when you're actually outside, you won't have to clean up dried beans off the floor like we would if said indoor sensory bin gets tipped over. Instead, we just take the messy clothes off at the door and put the kids in the tub, because while kids get dirty out there, kids can also be washed!

Kids can be their own guide and we want to encourage that freedom to explore rather than step in to "entertain" or direct them. We trust that in those moments when they are staring at, enjoying, and studying a tiny beetle on their own, our commentary isn't needed. Rather than jump in and be a distraction with a "What color is that beetle?" or "How many legs does that have?" we can just be available for questions if they have any and respect their concentration at that moment with our silence. Moments in nature are the perfect time to practice trusting the child as a competent being capable of following their own interests.

If however, the child seems to be open to some ideas outside, I've got a few to offer in Part 4 of the book.

"'Wait while observing.' That is the motto for the educator. Let us wait, and be always ready to share in both the joys and the difficulties which the child experiences."

—MARIA MONTESSORI

155

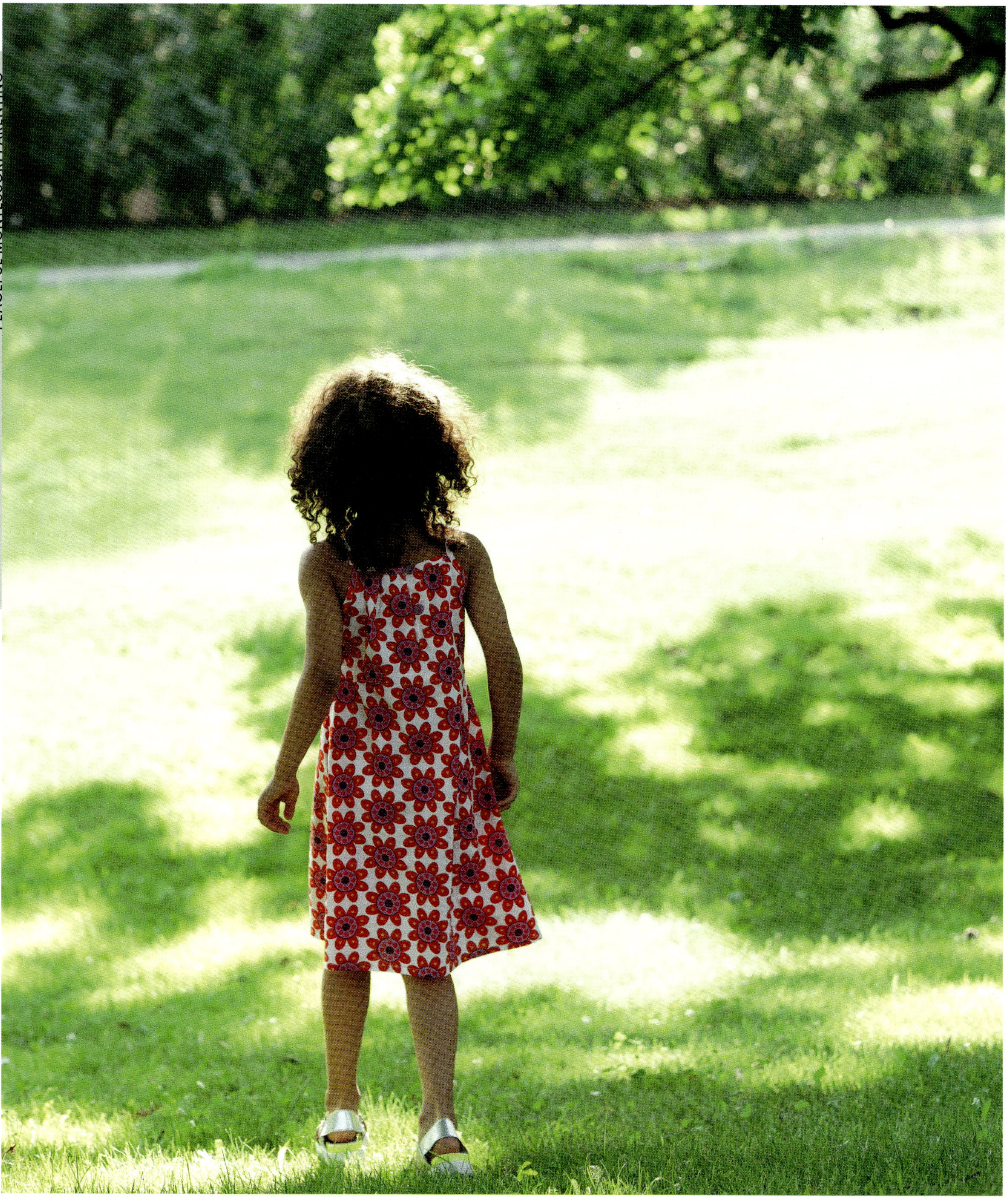

The Child-Led Walk

In the Montessori approach, a child-led walk is a deliberate and thoughtful exploration of the outdoors where the child takes charge of the journey. Before leaving the house, a parent's job is to set our intention of patience and honor the child's pace, interests, and personal goals on the walk. You'd be surprised how difficult this is—to slow down and be present is a big contrast to the usual day-to-day for most modern-day adults. In the child-led walk, the adult has a perfect opportunity to see the world through the child's eyes, unhurried and ever-present as kids naturally are. We offer support when needed, but let the child's curiosity steer the way. It's a brilliant way to nurture autonomy, independence, and a deep connection to nature. As the child meanders through the outdoor wonders, they engage their senses, observe the intricacies of the environment, and naturally cultivate a love for learning. While we love a little trail hike, the benefit is the same when you simply walk around the neighborhood. This approach isn't just about a stroll. It's a holistic experience that embraces the Montessori philosophy—letting the child lead their own exploration and, in doing so, fostering a genuine appreciation for the world around them.

Find your balance in child-led walks and parent-led walks. Stroller rides every day are truly a sanity saver. Walking at my speed while the kids rest their little bodies in the stroller is also beneficial to all if it helps you feel good and show up as the parent you want to be. Modeling a healthy and active lifestyle with a parent who prioritizes the needs of all bodies in the family (including our own) is a gift to them. Consider the time of day when either walk would be best suited. We personally find child-led walks are best in the morning hours and stroller walks are great for that late afternoon stretch when everyone is a bit tired and in need of fresh air.

"We must let the child walk and notice how he walks. His legs are short in comparison to ours and therefore he walks more slowly. Not only this, but the child explores the environment. The attention of little children is continually being drawn to one thing or other on their walks. They stop to observe and admire things they see."

—MARIA MONTESSORI, THE 1946 LONDON LECTURES

The Garden

In the Montessori home, having a garden isn't just about growing plants; it's like cultivating a little haven for holistic development. The garden becomes an extension of the learning environment, offering tons of benefits. First off, there's the hands-on experience—kids get down and dirty, planting seeds, observing growth, and understanding the cycle of life. It's a living classroom, teaching them responsibility, patience, and a deep connection to nature. The garden is also a treasure trove for sensory exploration—feeling the soil, smelling the flowers, and listening to the rustle of leaves. Beyond that, there's the joy of harvesting homegrown goodies, fostering a sense of accomplishment, respect, and a healthy relationship with food. Plus, a garden is a subtle yet powerful teacher of environmental stewardship, instilling in kids the importance of caring for the Earth. So, in a Montessori home, a garden isn't just a patch of green; it's a vibrant, hands-on learning space that nurtures curiosity, responsibility, and a lifelong love for the natural world.

A caveat to add here: If it's going to spread you too thin and be more stress than joy, then it's not the time to make a garden. If you are interested and want to start small, a few potted veggies or fruit will be amazing!

I've always wanted a garden, so even when we lived in the city, and more easily now that we have a little more land, we've always found a way to grow even a few things. It's taken a lot to release the idea that I was born with a naturally black thumb and to just keep on keeping on; practicing, learning, and persevering through the challenges. This is a true gift for kids to see and experience, as well. Gardening isn't easy and there's a lot out of our hands—heat, cold, rain, drought, hungry bunnies and beetles, or plants getting sick. I had no idea it would be so tricky!

I also had no idea that it would be so joyful. From spring to fall, our kids rush outside first thing in the morning to look for new blooms and harvests. From finding adorable sleeping bees in the flowers (this is a real thing!), to tasting new flavors fresh from the vine, spotting hummingbirds, and admiring the sparkle of dew drops in the sunlight, I often feel like the garden is a little utopia for them. When our friends visit, those kids, too, spend most of their time in the garden.

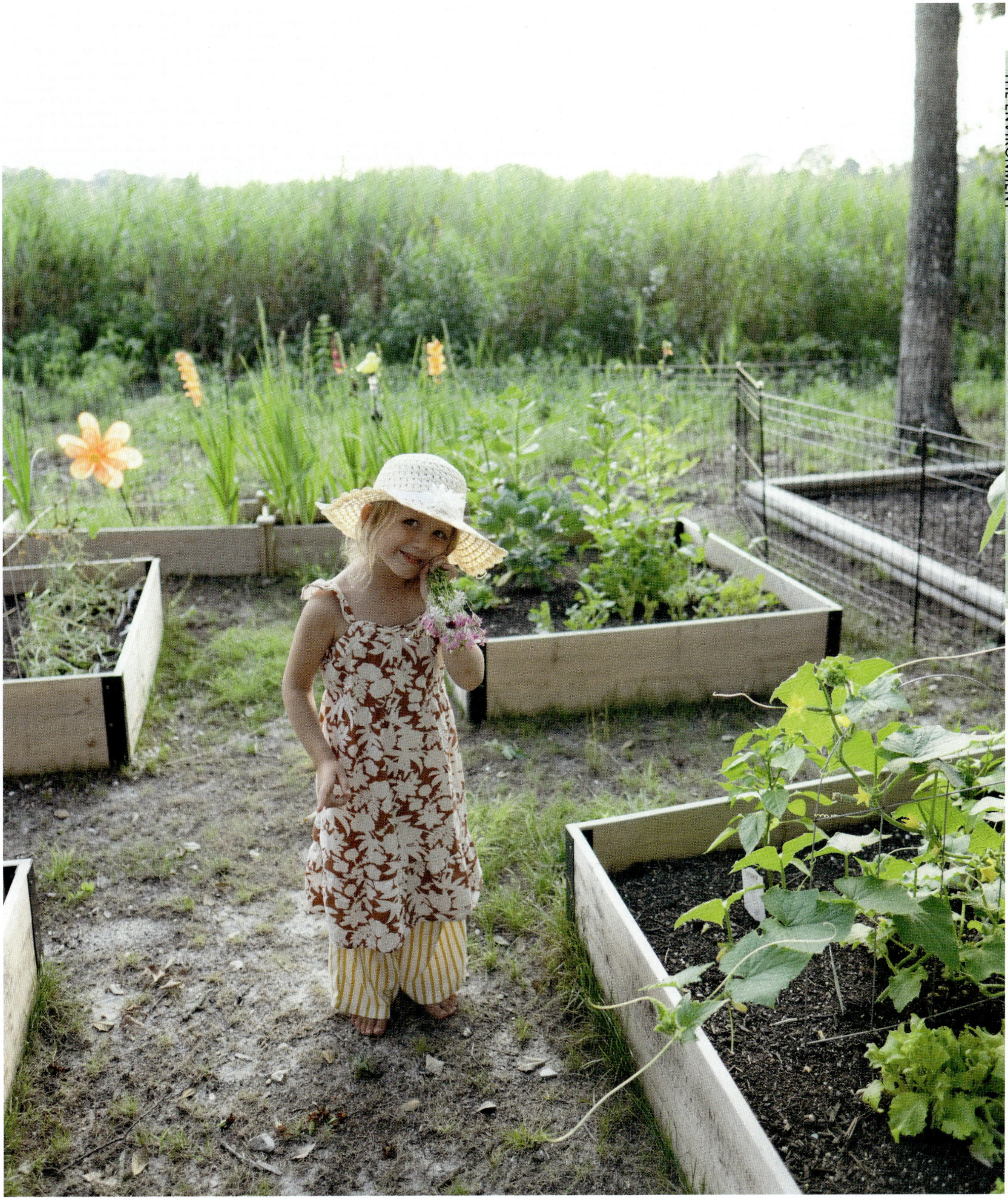

From the earliest baby days of peaceful moments sitting in nature; to toddlers digging, watering, harvesting, and learning; to preschool age and up studying, planning, and taking a big role—there's something for every age in the garden.

Just getting started? Here are steps to guide you through the process, considering factors like your garden zone, plant compatibility, and involving kids:

- **Understand Your Garden Zone:** Research your USDA hardiness zone to understand the climate and conditions specific to your area. This helps in selecting plants that thrive in your region.

- **Choose Kid-Friendly Plants:** Opt for plants that are easy to grow and engage children's senses. Examples include sunflowers, cherry tomatoes, strawberries, and herbs like mint or basil.

- **Plan the Garden Layout:** Consider the sunlight requirements of plants and arrange them accordingly. Involve kids in the planning process, discussing where each plant will go and why.

- **Teach Plant Compatibility:** Explain the concept of companion planting to kids, which is how certain plants benefit each other by deterring pests or enhancing growth. For example, planting marigolds near tomatoes can help repel certain insects.

- **Involve Kids in Soil Preparation:** Model how to prepare the soil by loosening it with a small shovel or trowel. Discuss the importance of good soil for plant growth.

- **Planting Seeds or Seedlings:** Let kids take an active role in planting seeds or seedlings. Teach them about seed depth, watering needs, and the importance of giving plants enough space to grow.

- **Watering Routine:** Establish a watering routine and involve kids in this essential task. Teach them how to water the base of the plants, avoiding the leaves, and explain the role of water in plant growth. Consider venturing into rain water collection as a source for your garden.

- **Monitoring Growth:** Encourage kids to observe and track the growth of their plants. Discuss the changes they notice, from sprouting leaves to the appearance of flowers and fruits. We love bringing a measuring tape out and recording from sprout to fully grown.

- **Weeding and Mulching:** Teach kids how to identify and safely remove weeds. Additionally, involve them in the process of adding mulch around plants to retain moisture and suppress weeds.

- **Harvesting and Enjoying Fruits:** When the time comes, involve kids in the exciting process of harvesting. Show them how to pick fruits or vegetables gently and discuss the rewards of their efforts—enjoying the homegrown produce.

- **Extend Learning:** Use the garden as an ongoing learning opportunity. Discuss the life cycle of plants, pollination, and the role of beneficial insects. Consider keeping a gardening journal with kids to document observations and experiences.

By involving kids in each step of the gardening process, you not only create a beautiful and productive garden but also foster a sense of responsibility, curiosity, and a lifelong connection to nature.

4
Montessori Work

In Montessori philosophy, the term "work" is used to describe the activities children engage in within the carefully prepared Montessori environment. Now, it might sound a bit unusual to call what looks like play "work," but there's fascinating reasoning behind it. See, in Montessori education, the activities are designed to be purposeful and meaningful, aligning with the child's developmental stage.

WORK AS PLAY

Activities for kids aren't just about keeping them busy; they're intentionally crafted to stimulate various aspects of their growth—cognitive, physical, and emotional. So, calling it "work" reflects the respect for the child's innate desire to actively explore, learn, and contribute to their own development. The question we always hear is, "Well, is 'work' just play, then?" There are a number of paradigms when it comes to this. Paradigms that say, "Work is play," or "Play isn't work," or maybe "Work needs play." They all have their own reasoning and in each of them the Montessori educational pedagogy still stands strong.

Many Montessori views today often argue that Montessori would recognize work as play. All the many forms of play have benefits in childhood and can be offered in the prepared environment.

Don't let the term fool you—a child's "work" isn't about pressure or formal tasks. It's about creating an environment where children can naturally engage in hands-on learning experiences. The idea is to instill a sense of responsibility, independence, and concentration in the child. Dr. Montessori said, "The child who concentrates is immensely happy," and anyone who observes a child absorbed in even the simplest of work, like washing their own small table, can see the pride in themselves and the joy in their little hearts.

Through the carefully curated environment, all work is that of joy and their own intrinsic interest. When we peel that back to the underlying message about what "work" is, then we have to consider the profound long-term impact this has on children.

Work is valuable, respected, held to a certain regard, *and* it's often spoken of as something only adults get to do. If you work from home, you likely set the precedent that during your work time, your space is to be respected and there cannot be interruptions. In the same way, when a child is working, we respect them and honor their concentration—sending the message that they are valued and significant, as well. As functioning members of society, they'll also be expected to join the workforce one day; by laying the foundation that work is joyful, a great opportunity for feeding our interests, and helps us to grow in so many ways, we set the tone for a child who values work, not dreads it. As the child of a single mother who could barely ever scrape by with multiple jobs, one of the most profound lessons in life I learned

"Respect all reasonable forms of activity in which the child engages and try to understand them."

—MARIA MONTESSORI

from her was a better mindset around work. She told us this: "Do what you *love,* so that your passion drives you to work hard, and with that drive, the money will follow." A child who ultimately chooses a career they enjoy because they've been led to it through their own inner guide after a childhood of exploring what feels like *them* is such a privilege, and one that I hope every child can experience.

So, in a nutshell, in the Montessori world, "work" is a term that reflects the intentional, purposeful, and engaging nature of the activities designed to support a child's holistic development. It's a bit of a linguistic quirk that carries a world of thoughtful educational philosophy behind it. Through personal observation, I encourage you to notice the value a child places on their own activities when we acknowledge it as work. Little toddlers explaining that they need a moment to continue their "work," and the pride on their faces as we respect their process, will never cease to fill my heart.

I think the most important thing that I can say here is that the activities, materials, aligned toys, etc. are all the cherry on top, as far as the needs of the child go. The priorities in a child's development go as follows:

- Fed and safe, with basic needs met

- Secure and healthy attachment with a loving caregiver who thinks the sun sets and rises just for them

- An environment that fosters independence, while holding boundaries where needed

- And then, Montessori work

While we want to give our kids all there is to offer, we have to remember to keep it appropriate and keep our priorities set. If we put all our effort into activity after activity, raising a kid who's high achieving in math, reading, and more, but can't regulate their emotions, none of that academic stuff is really going to matter.

EQ (emotional intelligence) is considered more notable than IQ in relation to "success" in careers. IQ will, of course, get you to a certain level of your career, but to truly move up the ladder, a Harvard study (among others) found a higher relation to emotional intelligence. While kids are in this beautiful, absorbent early stage of development, we invite them to learn organically from their environment, the outdoors, their relationships, and their inner feelings—that foundation guides them later when we start looking at their "academic success."

So, whether you're following Montessori for the child's education or not, know that the foundation you're laying with all the rest of this peaceful Montessori lifestyle is what's truly shaping those minds long term.

WHAT DEFINES MONTESSORI "WORK"?

For an activity to be considered Montessori aligned, it typically adheres to a few fundamental principles. While there isn't a strict checklist, several key elements are commonly present in Montessori-aligned work:

- **Hands-On and Sensorial:** Montessori activities are designed to be hands-on and engage the senses. Materials often have a tactile component, allowing children to explore and learn through the five senses.

- **Purposeful and Meaningful:** The activities have a clear purpose and are selected based on the developmental needs and interests of the child. Each activity is intended to foster one concept at a time. This is an easy way to spot whether a toy being advertised as "Montessori" is actually Montessori at all. For instance, those "Montessori" busy boards are quite misaligned, as there are so many concepts in just one material. The child will struggle to focus, repeat, and master new skills with so many things there intended to "busy" them.

- **Self-Directed Learning:** Montessori emphasizes the child's role in directing their own learning and fostering independence. The material is thoughtfully presented in a way that allows them to complete the work without an adult. You'll usually find work in a basket or tray that contains everything needed.

- **Control of Error:** The principle of "control of error" serves as a key feature within learning materials. It functions as a discreet mechanism embedded in these materials, allowing children to autonomously identify and remedy their own mistakes. Imagine a child immersed in a Montessori work, whether arranging the pink tower or manipulating geometric shapes. Within these materials lies a deliberate design where errors in the child's work are visibly evident, eliminating the constant need for adult intervention. The child, upon recognizing a mistake, takes the initiative to correct it independently. Beyond serving as a corrective tool, control of error embodies a profound aspect of self-reflection, encouraging children to learn from both successful outcomes and missteps. This is a foundational principle in Montessori education, nurturing independence, building confidence, and instilling a genuine passion for the learning process from the earliest stages of education. As a Montessori guide, we're able to let the material "correct" the child rather than having to take on that role ourselves.

- **Promotes Focus:** Montessori work builds interest in a way that invites the child to repeat the work over and over again. Through repetition, the child is on their way to mastery of new skills and concepts, while honoring their individual pace.

While these elements are often present in Montessori-aligned activities, it's essential to note that the true essence of Montessori lies in understanding and embodying the principles rather than adhering to a rigid checklist. The philosophy is flexible and adaptable to various cultural and educational contexts while staying true to the core values of respecting the child and supporting their natural development.

Maria Montessori created didactic learning materials, but she didn't make toys. So, any toys you see advertised as Montessori that fit into these guidelines would be "Montessori-aligned" toys, not "Montessori." Just helpful to know!

Also, a note on fantasy play. Montessori emphasizes the importance of grounding children in reality to help them first understand and navigate the world around them before engaging in fantasy play. Why is this? Until around age five or six, children have a lot of difficulty distinguishing between "real" and fantasy, which makes it very confusing and often scary for them. While we respect their forms of play and imagination, we're honest about what's real or not real, while limiting their exposure to fantasy.

DECIDING WHAT TO OFFER

Have you ever scrolled through Pinterest, found an activity that looked cool, and done all the prep to offer it to your child—only to see them spend 3 seconds with it, and you're left with a huge mess to clean up? You're not alone! This happens. It can be disheartening, though, and we want to minimize the frustration of the aimless scroll and offer work that will actually pique their interests. The way to do that, and much more, is through observation.

"Observe more,
do less,
enjoy most."

—MAGDA GERBER

HOW TO SENSITIVELY OBSERVE

While research and expert teachings are useful, truly knowing a child requires observing them with a sense of wonder rather than certainty. This shift in perspective enhances our understanding and creates a more responsive relationship tailored to each child's unique needs.

Observing your children the Montessori way involves a thoughtful and respectful approach to understanding their needs, interests, and developmental stages. Here are some tips:

1. **Unbusy Your Body and Mind:** Observation, with practice, can be a meditative practice that truly opens us up to see the wonder and magic of our children.

2. **Observe Without Interruption:** When observing your children, try to do so without interrupting their activities and without anything interrupting you (phone, email, etc.) Sit quietly and attentively, allowing them to engage in their tasks without feeling observed or pressured.

   You might begin your observation once you've noticed they are in a work flow and engaging in the prepared environment. You'll absolutely find me hiding behind the doorway, peeking in sneakily to make some notes.

   It works out well to spend ten minutes of quality time first and then announce that you are going to observe them: "I'm going to sit and watch you work. I love watching and learning more about you!" This is also a lovely connection builder. Consider how special you feel when those you love show up to watch you doing something you love and work hard at.

3. **Take Notes:** What do you see? Remember to observe and note objectively. For example: "I see my child pulling his books off the shelf. He lingers on one cover—it's a book about animals. He spends 5 minutes pointing to and saying animal names." Avoid assumptions like, "He loves animals!" Such things will come at your hypothesis stage. For now, keep it matter-of-fact and clear. Note any patterns or milestones you observe, as well as any areas where your child may need additional support or encouragement.

4. **Use Active Listening:** Pay close attention to what your child is saying and doing. Listen actively to their words and observe their actions, noting their interests, strengths, and challenges.

5. **Reflect:** We want to hypothesize now and get curious about ways we can better support them. Are they in a sensitive period for language? Can we offer more language materials? Is the environment meeting their needs? Did you notice your child had to walk back and forth over and over to bring two materials together that could easily be moved for a better workflow? Would it be better to move her table closer to the shelf? Or further? Maybe it's getting in the way. Did she not touch the dinosaurs for two weeks in a row? Maybe it's time to rotate this out for something that meets her needs and interests more. This is your time to translate what you observed to be sure that the environment and materials are, in fact, meeting your child's needs.

By observing your children in a sensitive and respectful way, you can gain valuable insights into their needs, interests, and development, allowing you to better support them on their Montessori journey.

SENSITIVE PERIODS

What should you do with your observations? Expand! Through her years of study and observation, Maria Montessori discovered what she called "sensitive periods." These periods are characterized by intense focus and interest in specific aspects of their environment.

During their sensitive period, kids pick up certain skills easily. They're super into it, almost like they can't get enough. But once this phase is over, that intense interest fades away and won't be returning. It doesn't mean they can't learn those skills later, though. It just means they'll have to put in a bit more effort to get the hang of them.

"Children pass through definite periods in which they reveal psychic aptitudes and possibilities which afterward disappear. That is why, at particular epochs of their life, they reveal an intense and extraordinary interest in certain objects and exercises, which one might look for in vain at later age."

—MARIA MONTESSORI

Knowing these periods exist offers us some big clues on what our children will likely enjoy and be drawn to at a specific age and stage. Here are the sensitive periods Montessori identified for ages one through six:

- **Order:** Around ages one through five, children often show a strong preference for orderliness and predictability. They may enjoy arranging objects in a particular sequence or organizing their environment in a specific way.

- **Movement:** From birth to around age four-and-a-half, children have a natural inclination toward movement and physical activity. They may be drawn to activities that allow them to explore their physical abilities and refine their motor skills.

- **Language:** Between birth and six years old, children experience a sensitive period for language development. They are highly receptive to learning new words and may begin to use language to express themselves more effectively.

- **Refinement of the Senses:** From birth to five, children go through a sensitive period for refining their senses. They become increasingly aware of subtle differences in sensory stimuli and may seek out activities that stimulate their senses.

- **Social Behaviors:** Around ages two-and-a-half to six, children start to become more interested in social interactions and relationships. They may seek out opportunities to engage with peers and develop important social skills such as sharing and cooperation.

- **Small Objects:** Between ages one and three, children are especially drawn to exploring tiny items, which helps them develop fine motor skills and a keen attention to detail.

By recognizing and nurturing these sensitive periods, we help our kids thrive.

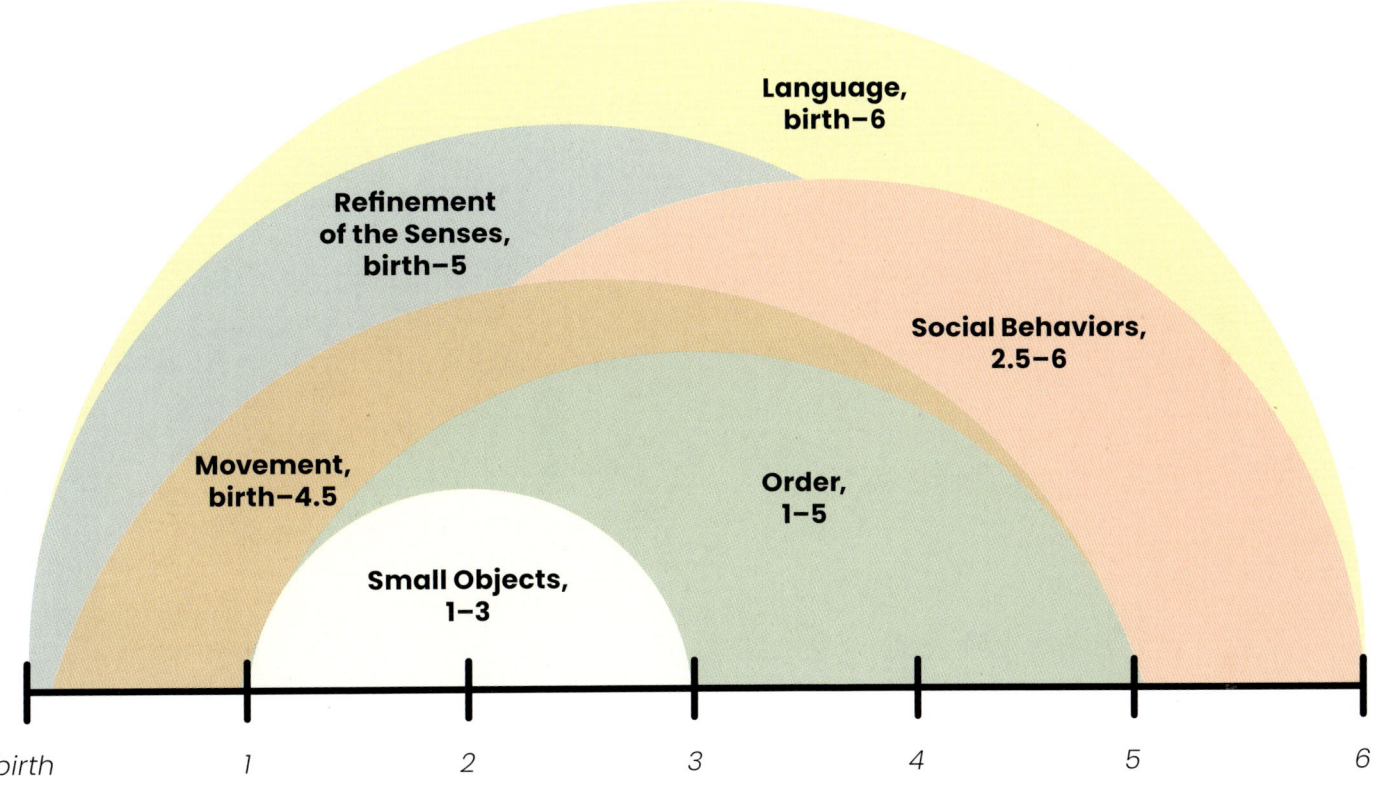

MONTESSORI SENSITIVE PERIODS

Birth to 6

SCHEMAS

Another great tool is something called "schemas." Though not traditionally Montessori, we can consider the theory aligned, and goodness—does it help!

Schemas are repetitive patterns of behavior that children engage in during early childhood, typically between the ages of one and six. These behaviors reflect the child's efforts to make sense of the world around them and to explore and understand concepts and ideas. Here are some common schemas observed in early childhood, along with examples of activities that support each schema:

Transporting: Children are fascinated with moving objects from one place to another.

- Provide baskets or containers for children to carry objects around.
- Set up toy vehicles or doll strollers for children to push around the room.
- Offer materials for building structures that can be moved from one location to another.

Rotation: Children enjoy spinning objects or themselves, as well as twisting and turning things.

- Provide tops, spinning toys, or fidget spinners for children to explore rotation.
- Offer materials for children to twist and turn, such as pipe cleaners or clay.
- Create opportunities for children to experiment with rotating objects in water or sand.

Trajectory: Children are interested in the path or trajectory of objects, such as throwing, dropping, or rolling.

- Provide balls or bean bags for children to throw into targets or containers.
- Set up ramps or slides for children to roll objects down.
- Provide water play—children enjoy pouring and dumping water, and sitting in the tub as it fills up to enjoy the running water from the faucet.
- Offer materials for children to experiment with dropping objects from different heights.

Enclosure/Enveloping: Children like to hide, cover, or enclose themselves or objects.

- Provide tents, tunnels, or large boxes for children to crawl into or hide under.
- Offer blankets or scarves for children to use in imaginative play, such as building forts or wrapping up toys.
- Create opportunities for children to explore nesting toys or containers that fit inside each other.

Connecting: Children are interested in joining objects together or connecting parts.

- Provide building blocks, magnetic tiles, or construction toys for children to connect and build with.
- Offer materials for children to string together, such as beads or pasta.
- Create opportunities for children to explore puzzles or interlocking toys.

Transforming: Children enjoy changing the form or appearance of objects through manipulation or construction.

- Provide materials for open-ended art activities, such as clay, paint, or collage materials.
- Offer loose parts or found objects for children to use in creative construction projects.
- Create opportunities for children to experiment with pouring, mixing, or molding materials like sand, water, or dough.

Between sensitive periods and schemas, we have so much information on how to make educated and intentional choices in the activities, materials, and opportunities we offer kids!

By stepping into this version of ourselves as parents who choose to sensitively observe our children, not just to boost independent work cycles, but to better understand them, we're making a profound decision—a decision to see our kids with curious compassion. It's in the mindset you've cultivated to see their throwing as a trajectory schema, which begs for more opportunity to explore that need to throw and learn. And it's in the heart of empathy and the gentle hug you extend to them as they scream and cry over that blue cup, knowing that they are good, pure, amazing humans who are showing us they need our help to uncover the need beneath the behavior. In every moment that we choose compassionate curiosity, what we're really saying to our children is: You are important, you matter, you are a priority, and I'm here to love you unconditionally. Never for one moment doubt the value of a parent showing up for a child in this way. Having someone who sees us—I mean *truly* sees us—is the gift of a lifetime, and one that every child deserves.

PRESENTING MONTESSORI WORK

Presenting an activity in the Montessori way is a thoughtful process that respects and nurtures a child's natural desire to learn. Here are some key tips for effectively presenting a Montessori activity:

1. **Organize Materials Thoughtfully:** Montessori materials should be organized in a clear, orderly, and accessible manner. Each item should have its specific place on the shelf, arranged from the simplest to the most complex, typically *left to right,* mirroring the way we read. This order helps the child to develop a sense of organization and sequence in their learning.

2. **Use a Tray:** In a tray, the child is able to find all contents of a specific work, set in an "undone" manner that invites the child's interest. Like shelf organization, the materials in a tray are set up from order of use, left to right.

3. **Preparation and Mindfulness:** Before presenting, ensure that you are calm and focused. Prepare the environment to be free from distractions, ensuring that the space is quiet, clean, and inviting. Model your intentional hand positioning on the tray as you bring the materials to the work space, often defined by a work mat or table. Invite the child to join you in a new work presentation.

4. **Positioning and Proximity:** Sit next to or slightly in front of the child, on their dominant side. This position allows the child to see your movements clearly without having to turn their head excessively. It also makes it easier for the child to mimic your actions.

5. **S-H-O-W:** This acronym stands for Slow Hands Omit Words. Keep this in mind when presenting anything new to children. Here's why:

   Demonstrating with slow, deliberate movements allows the child to observe and process each step clearly. The precision in your movements helps to focus the child's attention and illustrates the care and respect for the materials.

   Using minimal language during the presentation keeps the focus on the actions, not the words. This approach helps the child to concentrate on the movements and the purpose of the material, rather than being distracted by excessive verbal instructions.

6. **Child's Turn:** After demonstrating, invite the child to try the activity. This invitation should be gentle and respectful, allowing the child to feel a sense of ownership over their learning process.

7. **Observation Without Interruption:** Once the child begins the activity, observe without interruption. This observation is crucial to assess their understanding, interest, and to provide guidance if necessary. However, we're not jumping in to correct them; rather, we want to allow the child to explore and learn independently. It may be right to ask the child if you may have one more turn, and take the opportunity to model with S-H-O-W in mind again. Or you may find it better to wait until another time and present the material again, after noting areas the child needs support. Remember: Teach by teaching, not by correcting.

8. **Respect the Child's Pace:** Offer time and space for the child to work at their pace. This respect for their rhythm fosters deeper engagement and understanding.

9. **Encourage Independence:** Encourage the child to prepare their workspace, perform the activity, and then tidy up afterward. This full cycle of activity fosters independence, responsibility, and respect for the learning environment.

While it's valuable to know how to present in the Montessori way, it's also important to remember that your home isn't a classroom. It's possible that your child may not be willing or able to "listen" to you the way they can their school teacher, or there may be more distractions at home than a classroom. If the child loses interest mid-lesson, know that this can be typical in the early years and it doesn't mean that they didn't absorb what you've presented. If that's the case, it may not be the right time of day for a presentation, might not be developmentally appropriate work, or they're just not into it. You know your child best! Presentations don't just happen at the shelf; they happen all throughout the day in raising kids. There are opportunities all around. It's as simple as using S-H-O-W with teeth brushing, using the whisk while making dinner, painting, and so much more.

PRACTICAL LIFE

Montessori practical life work is fundamental in Montessori. It's all about helping children learn how to take care of themselves and their environment, fostering independence, coordination, concentration, and a sense of responsibility. We find that this area of work in particular is a huge booster in a child's feelings of significance and belonging—based on Alfred Adler's theories, this plays a giant role in a child's behavior. Lucky for us, practical life opportunities happen naturally all day long. I find it to be the easiest way to "Montessori," and it tends to be exactly what kids are begging us to have a chance to help with! To us, the "chores" can feel mundane, but to a child, it is their one-way ticket to feeling like a valued member of the family and they just love it. Here are the five areas of practical life work, their value, and examples of each:

Preliminary Exercises: Here, we work on all the basic movements of participating in society.

- Pouring
- Scooping
- Sitting in a chair
- Pushing a chair in
- Carrying a tray
- Turning pages in a book

Care of Self: This area focuses on activities that help children become more independent in looking after their own bodies. It's valuable for developing self-care skills, fostering independence, and building self-esteem.

- Dressing frames (for practicing buttons, zips, and ties)
- Hand washing
- Nose blowing
- Managing personal hygiene

Care of the Environment: These activities teach children to respect and take care of their surroundings. They instill a sense of responsibility, order, and pride in maintaining a clean, well-organized environment.

- Dusting
- Sweeping
- Watering plants
- Caring for classroom pets

Grace and Courtesy: This area is about teaching social skills and manners—crucial for smooth and respectful interactions in society. It promotes social awareness, empathy, and respect for others.

- Greeting others
- Saying "please" and "thank you"—taught by modeling rather than constantly prompting with "say please!"
- Table manners
- Practicing polite conversation

Control of Movement: This involves activities that help refine motor skills and coordination, and teach children to move with purpose and care. It's important for developing physical dexterity and spatial awareness.

- Walking on a line
- Carrying objects with care
- Balancing activities

This isn't just about mastering tasks, but also about learning to participate in and contribute to their community (your family, in this case). These activities are designed to be engaging and meaningful, reflecting real-life tasks that children observe in their daily lives. Practical life work generally invites lots of repetition, which brings the child tons of joy and is key to building concentration and mastering skills. Through practical life work, children build confidence, gain a sense of belonging, and develop the skills and attitudes necessary for a successful and harmonious life. It's interesting that toy companies make every version of "real life" into a toy for children, because we all know they are so drawn to the things that we grown-ups get to do. Maria Montessori found that children prefer the real thing. They want to have a chance to feel the satisfaction of eating a muffin that they made, have pride in their contributions, and take steps, every day, toward more autonomy.

Counting Sticks
3–6 y
page 180

Color Sorting
2–6 y
page 183

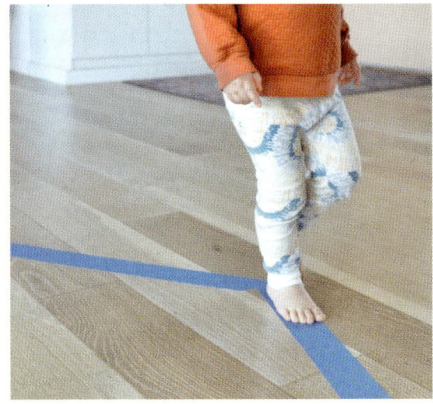

Walk the Line
2½–6 y
page 184

DIY Ball Run
1–6+ y
page 186

Five Senses Active Meditation
all ages
page 190

Big Breaths for Little Kids
1+ y
page 193

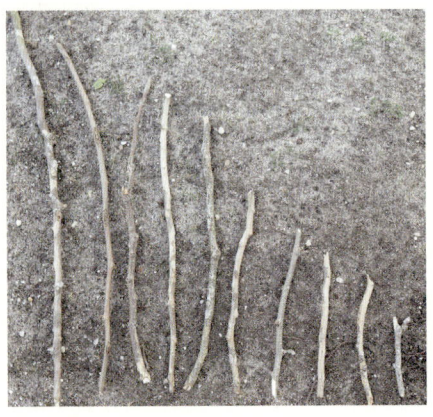

Stick Rod Maze
2+ y
page 196

Nature Scavenger Hunt
2+ y
page 200

The Mind Table
4+ y
page 203

Montessori-Aligned Activities

Here are a few of our favorite, simple,
low- or no-cost Montessori-aligned
activities and works.

COUNTING STICKS

This is a simple and interactive counting activity, based on the concept of the Montessori Spindles Box (181), that builds the concept of numbers and quantity. This activity not only teaches numerical concepts but also recycles materials and incorporates natural elements, aligning with environmental stewardship and Montessori principles. Win, win!

if	when	then
• The child has a basic under-standing of numbers and counting—can recognize or is working on recognizing numbers up to ten • Is interested in numbers and counting • Is collecting or sorting items	Three to six years old	Then offer this to: • Develop number recognition • Enhance fine motor skills as the child picks up and places twigs • Introduce basic math concepts of counting, one-to-one correspondence, and quantity • Encourage independent learning and problem-solving

Materials:

- 11 empty toilet paper rolls
- A sturdy piece of cardboard or tray
- Marker
- A collection of 55 small sticks or twigs, cleaned and dried
- Nontoxic glue or tape

Let's Do It!

1. Collect and clean the materials. Ensure you have enough twigs so that each number can be matched with the corresponding quantity of twigs. Cut the cardboard to a size that can comfortably fit all the toilet paper rolls.

2. Secure the empty toilet paper rolls onto the cardboard in a straight line using glue or tape, leaving a little space between each one to allow room for the child's hands to move freely.

3. Use a marker to label each toilet paper roll with numbers from 0 to 10. Note the Montessori version goes to 9, but we wanted to add one!

4. Prepare the twigs by ensuring they're all relatively the same length. Break or trim any that are too long.

5. Show the child the numbered rolls and explain that they will be filling each roll with the number of twigs that match the number on the roll.

6. Model how to do the activity by choosing a number, saying it out loud, and placing the corresponding number of twigs into the roll.

7. Invite the child to have a turn. Encourage them to start from 0 or 1 and work their way up to higher numbers, placing the correct number of twigs into each roll.

8. As the child places the twigs into the rolls, count along with them to reinforce number recognition and one-to-one correspondence.

9. After the child has filled all the rolls, review the numbers together, counting the twigs in each roll to ensure the quantities are correct. Leave time for the child to notice errors, as this material is self-correcting in that there are *exactly* enough sticks for the work.

COLOR SORTING

2–6 y

This activity is reminiscent of Montessori-style sensorial work, where children develop their ability to classify objects by color, enhancing their visual discrimination skills, fine-motor skills, and cognitive development through sorting and categorization.

if

- The child shows interest in colors, sorting, or searching

when

Two to six years old

then

Then offer this to:

- Develop color recognition skills
- Strengthen fine motor skills
- Practice sorting and classifying

Materials:

- An empty, clean egg carton
- Nontoxic paint in various colors
- Paintbrushes
- An assortment of small objects or natural items

Let's Do It!

1. Begin by inviting the child to help paint the carton, each compartment a different color, corresponding to the items you have or intend to collect.

2. Set the carton aside to dry.

3. Take the child on a nature walk to collect the items and sort them in the tray as you go. If outdoors isn't an option, invite the child to find small objects of differing color in the house!

4. Observe the child as they work, offering minimal intervention to allow for independent learning. The painted compartments act as a control of error, allowing the child to self-correct by matching the item colors to the compartment colors.

Extension Work

- *Use the activity to discuss the nature items, including their names, where they come from, and other characteristics.*
- *Provide various shades of the same color to introduce the concept of gradients and shades.*

Safety Note

Be aware of toxic-to-handle plants. Supervise the child at all times during the activity to prevent any potential choking hazards or contact with harmful substances.

183

WALK THE LINE

2½–6 y

This Montessori activity is one of the simplest set-ups, with a big impact on a child's development.

if	when	then

if

- Child is unable to refine movements, and you're noting "clumsiness" or lack of awareness
- Child has disorganized energy
- Child appears in need of a mindful moment

when

Two-and-a-half to six years old

then

Then offer this to:

- Improve their balance and coordination
- Learn to control their body movements and build spacial awareness
- Develop concentration and self-regulation skills

Materials:

- A long strip of tape (masking or painter's tape is ideal, as it is easy to remove) or a balance beam, or chalk for outdoor sidewalk or driveway
- Music player (optional, for walking to the rhythm)
- A bell or any object that requires careful movement to carry without making noise (optional, for advanced practice)

Let's Do It!

1. Preparation:

- Choose a quiet, open space either indoors or outdoors where a line can be laid out straight or in a simple shape.
- Place the tape on the floor to create a line that's easily visible and approximately 2 to 4 in. (5 to 10 cm) wide. If you're outside, you can use chalk.
- If you are using objects like a bell, place them near the start of the line.
- Set up your music player if you're using one, with calm, rhythmic music that's suitable for a walking pace.

2. Presentation:

- Introduce the activity to the child when they are calm and ready to focus.
- Show them the line and demonstrate how to walk the line slowly and carefully, placing the heel of one foot directly in front of the toes of the other foot.
- Invite the child to walk the line, watching their movements, and taking another turn to model again, if needed.
- Once the child is comfortable, you can introduce variations, such as walking on tiptoes, walking with arms outstretched, or carrying an object like a bell without ringing it, a glass of water without spilling, or play some music and ask the child to walk to the rhythm. If using tape, not chalk, you may introduce a blindfold to enhance sensory awareness with bare feet.

3. Mindful Closing:

- Discuss with the child how they felt while walking the line. Encourage them to describe their movements and how they managed to maintain their balance, promoting self-reflection and language development.

DIY BALL RUN

This upcycled cardboard project is quick and cheap to put together. A ball run invites children to gain a better understanding of spatial awareness: space, distance, and direction. They learn to predict where a ball will go and how it'll travel through the run, which helps develop their spatial reasoning skills. Their visual tracking, which is an early reading skill, is also working hard as they follow the ball from ramp to ramp.

if

- Child repeatedly throws things. This may be a ball, or maybe a less-throwing-friendly item (e.g., maybe they are throwing food). Many assume this is a "behavioral issue," when oftentimes, it's related to a need in development. Remember: Kids are little scientists and there's always a need beneath the behavior!

- Child is dropping objects. They enjoy dropping objects from different heights to see how they fall. For example, they might drop toys from a table or watch leaves fall from a tree.

- Child is pointing and following paths. They may point to and track the paths of moving objects, such as birds in the sky, cars on the road, or planes overhead.

- Child is showing lots of repetition. Children pretty much spell "mastery" as r-e-p-e-t-i-t-i-o-n. You may observe them doing the same action and watching its outcome repeatedly.

when

Ages one to six and up

One to Three Years Old:
- At this age, children are still developing fine motor skills and hand-eye coordination. Simple ball runs with large, easy-to-manipulate balls (such as soft foam balls or wooden balls) can be introduced. Supervision is crucial to ensure safety.

Three to Five Years Old:
- Preschoolers are more capable of engaging with complex ball runs. They can help set up the run, adjust components, and experiment with different ball sizes and trajectories.

School-Age Children (Six and Up):
- Older children can create more intricate and elaborate ball runs using a variety of materials.

then

Then offer this to:

- Develop problem-solving skills
- Strengthen visual tracking skills
- Encourage fine motor skills
- Foster curiosity and experimentation
- Strengthen concentration and focus
- Support early math concepts
- Nurture a love for learning: The hands-on, interactive nature of a ball run makes learning fun and engaging. Children are more likely to be motivated to explore and discover when it's presented in an enjoyable way—I think that's true for adults, too, isn't it?

Materials:

- Cardboard boxes (different sizes)
- Cardboard tubes (e.g., paper towel rolls)
- Scissors or box cutter
- Tape (packing tape or duct tape)
- Balls (marbles, ping pong balls, or small wooden balls)
- Optional: Decorative paper, glue, markers, stickers, paint, etc.

Let's Do It!

1. Prepare the boxes. Take the cardboard boxes and cut off the flaps from the tops and bottoms, leaving you with an open rectangular or square shape.

2. Cut slits. Cut 1/8" by 3" (3 mm x 7.6 cm) slits on each side. Vary positions to support the angle of each ramp.

3. Create ramps. Cut cardboard into various lengths to serve as ramps for the balls. Be sure they are the same width as your slits. Strategically cut openings for where the ball will drop onto the next ramp. Attach these ramps to the inside of the boxes using tape. Angle them in different directions to make your ball run more interesting. I also think it's helpful to add some tape around the edges of the cardboard, to avoid any too-sharp areas for little ones.

4. Test the run. Drop a ball at the top of your ball run and watch it navigate its way through the chutes and boxes. Make any adjustments necessary to ensure a smooth journey.

5. Decorate further (optional). If you'd like to add more artistic flair, cover the cardboard box with decorative paper, paint it, color on it, add stickers—whatever brings your little one creative joy in this process!

6. Play and experiment. Invite the child to experience the ball run with a simple demonstration of the work.

Extension Work

- *Offer different types of balls and observe how they roll through the run. Encourage them to make predictions about the ball's path and discuss the results.*
- *Introduce concepts of gravity and cause-and-effect as the child observes how the balls move through the run.*
- *Discuss concepts of speed and trajectory as they experiment with dropping the balls from different heights.*

Safety Note

Ensure all small parts and materials are kept out of reach of very young children to prevent choking hazards. Clean up any cardboard scraps and craft supplies after the activity.

FIVE SENSES ACTIVE MEDITATION

This is a peaceful process of noticing the world around us—the perfect invitation to slow down together! When we simply tell a child that they must sit still and be mindful, it doesn't actually result in a mindful child—rather a confused and agitated one. Guided meditations like this are how we meet that expectation gap and offer them the tools needed to create calm in their body while also having fun. By practicing mindfulness activities like this in moments of calm and connection, we make it possible for our children to be able to access "grounding" as an emotional regulation tool in times of distress. These tools need to be taught outside of the moment of dysregulation to be effective, while children are in a receptive learning state.

if

- The child is moving about from activity to activity
- There are signs of dysregulation
- The family could benefit from more intentional moments throughout the day

when

Ideal for all ages and in every stage of development

- Do consider the time of day where a moment of peaceful-ness could help set the tone for your family. Great times to offer this meditation may be right after breakfast to begin a joyful morning, when it's nearly time to settle down for rest time or naps, in the evening after a family walk to regulate the nervous systems, or any time of day that you've noticed a pattern of dysreg-ulation, like leading up to a tricky transition.

then

Then offer this to:

- Introduce children to the concept of mindfulness and being present in the moment
- Encourage children to engage their senses and observe the natural world around them
- Promote relaxation, sensory awareness, and a sense of wonder

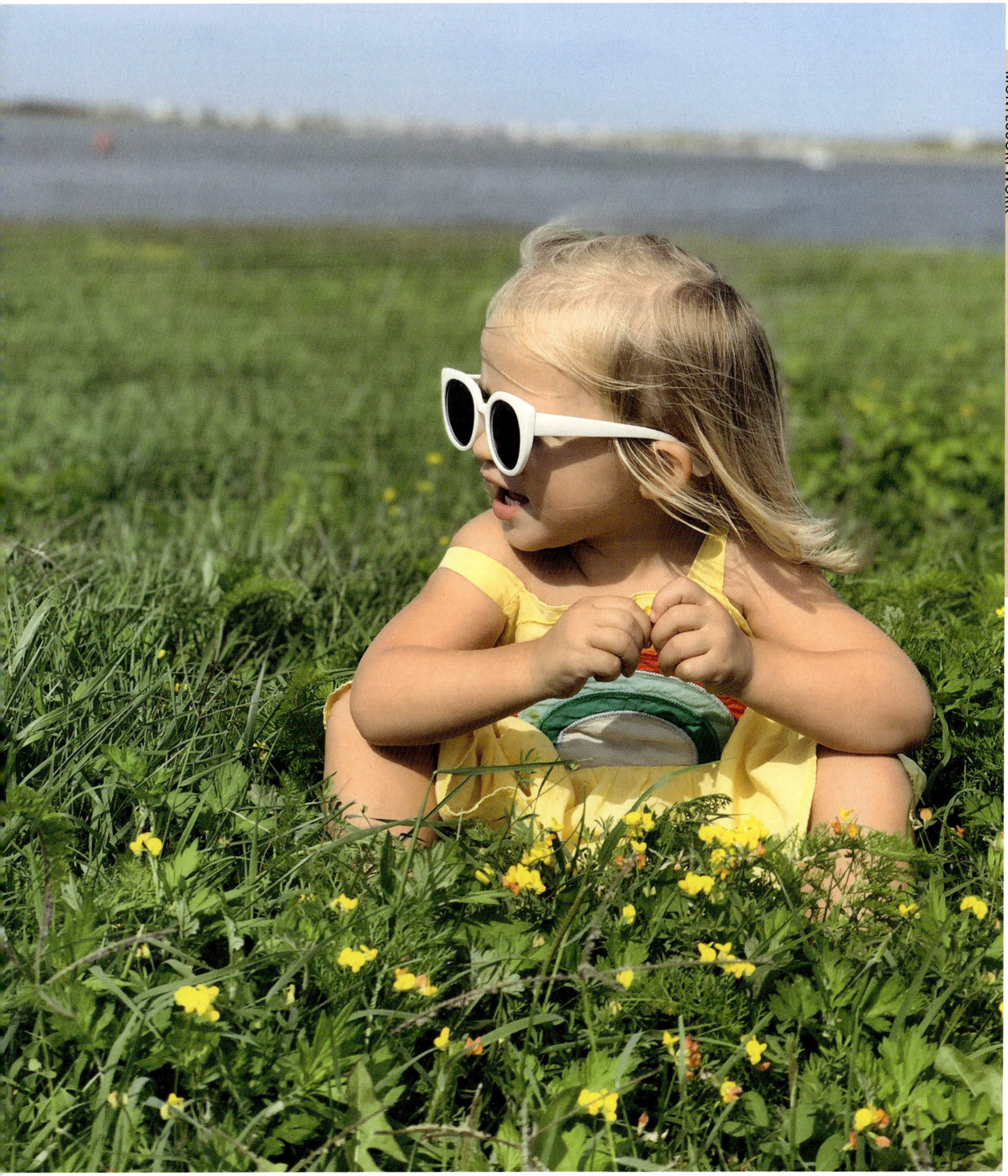

Materials:

- Outdoor space (such as a garden, park, or playground)
- A blanket or yoga mat (if you'd like, though, you can certainly just flop down onto the grass, dirt, or sand)

Let's Do It!

1. Find a comfortable spot to sit in nature.

2. Guide the meditation. For this activity, an easy rule of thumb is to ask for one observation of each of the senses per year of the child's life, up to five. For example: "Oh, my little two-year-old, would you like to come sit with me? Let's keep our bodies ever so still, like a rock. My body is so peaceful here. Let's fill our bellies with air and then let it out. What lovely views! I see a cloud and some birds. Two things! What are two things you see?"

3. Then, invite them through the list of senses.

   - See: Simply identify anything you see. Keep it simple or take it up a notch and invite them to observe and try to find something that they hadn't first noticed.
   - Hear: Listen carefully. What are the sounds that you hear? Recognize even the smallest buzz in the air.
   - Feel: How are you feeling internally, and what can you feel externally?
   - Smell: Take a deep breath in through your nose. What scents do you smell?
   - Taste: What are you tasting? Is it sweet, sour, or bitter? (It's optional to eat or drink during this time.)

4. Mindful closing.

   - Thank the children for participating.
   - Invite them to share how they felt during the meditation. "My body felt so calm and peaceful during this mediation. Do you notice anything your body is feeling right now?"
   - Emphasize the value of using their senses and being present in everyday life.
   - Let them know that mindfulness is a wonderful way to connect with nature and themselves.

Extension Work

If interested and age appropriate, invite children to collect some of the objects they noticed during the meditation for a closer look. This may include simply talking about textures, colors, or smells of each object, making observations notes together, leaf rubbings, nature collages, or simple paintings. These extensions allow them to further express their observations and creativity.

BIG BREATHS FOR LITTLE KIDS

This activity is a joyful and mindful exploration of how to engage in deep, calming breaths. A child doesn't automatically know how to take a deep breath. It actually requires support and teaching on our end to guide them in the type of breath that truly calms the mind and body. Just as adults benefit greatly from breathwork training, we can get our kids started on the right foot and guide them on how to access those deep, nervous-system-state-altering breaths. As with all mindfulness and "calm down" tools, these need to be taught and practiced outside of the moment of distress, so that those neural connections are strengthened and this tool becomes actually accessible to them! There are a few great ways to teach this, so grab what you have from around the house out of the options below and you can get started.

if

- The child has difficulty calming down
- There are signs of dysregulation
- The child would benefit from more intentional moments throughout the day

when

One year and up

then

Then offer this to:

- Add an element of fun and clear guidance as you guide the child in calming breaths
- Encourage children to engage in the tools available to stimulate the vagus nerve and activate the relaxation response of the parasympathetic (rest and digest) nervous system

Materials (Options):

- Flower
- Candle
- Bubbles
- Bubble bath
- Stuffed animals

Let's Do It!

Begin by creating a playful environment and gather the materials you choose. Explain that you feel like your body needs a moment of calm and you know just what to do for it!

1. Model taking a slow, deep breath in through your nose. Put a hand on your abdomen as you notice your belly rise with the breath in. See below for individual pointers depending on the chosen material.

2. On exhale, emphasize a long, deep release of the air.

3. Invite the child. "Oh, that feels peaceful in my body. Here you go, love, would you like to try?" If the child isn't ready to try themselves, remember that's okay. Model a few more times on your own to increase interest and then let them know you will help them whenever they are ready to give it a try.

- Smell a beautiful flower. Try to make the petals blow a bit with the wind of your exhale for an added visual.

- Blow out the candle. Just be sure to make a safety note like this, "Oh, that feels peaceful in my body. I'll light the candle for you too. The flame is very hot—only mama can light a candle and be sure to keep everyone safe while we practice this. Here you go, love, would you like to try?"

- Blowing bubbles. Explore the different speeds and strengths of exhalation, noting that a slow, deep, and mindful push of air will make the most bubbles! This is exactly the exhale we're looking for in a calming breath.

- Blowing bubbles in the bath. Take that big breath in, try to hold for one count, and release the air with force! See how many bath bubbles you can clear with your breath.

Remember, the key is to keep it light, enjoyable, and tailored to their interests. By turning deep breathing into a playful activity, you're helping them build a valuable skill for managing emotions and stress in a fun way. Practicing this outside of those moments of dysregulation, the child will be more likely to access these calming breaths, with a little help from you at first. In the moment, we can use imaginary bubbles or flowers, pulling from the real-life experience they got to enjoy with you. I love the reminder for kids to "Smell the flower," or "Blow the bubble"!

Also Try: Breathing Buddies

Invite the child to lie down on their back while you place a stuffed animal on their chest. As they breathe in and out, the child can observe the rhythmic movement of the stuffed animal, giving a visual of how big those breaths are by how far the stuffy rises and settles. This practice encourages them to be present, focusing solely on their breath. Adding this in for just a few minutes a day before transitions to school or bedtime can help in a major way. Using a visual timer can also help them grasp the short time commitment involved.

STICK ROD MAZE

Here we have nature's version of the Montessori Red Rods Maze. This is a perfect example of taking a classic sensorial Montessori material and getting all the great learning benefits for free! The Red Rods are a series of ten red, wooden rods 2.5 cm wide and 2.5 cm high (1 in. by 1 in.), whose length increases by 10 cm (3.9 in.) with each successive rod, making various lengths as shown. Our goal is to mimic this concept with sticks!

if

- You notice an interest in measuring, sorting, collecting, or all of the above
- The child would benefit from a calm and mindful work
- The child is bumping into things/needs some refinement in careful movements and spatial awareness

when

Ages two and up

then

Then offer this to:

- Distinguish differences in length, refining their visual perception and discrimination skills
- Help children develop a sense of order and understand the concept of length, called "size grading"
- Support the development of spatial awareness and reasoning, understanding how objects and their own body relate to each other in terms of position and distance
- Lay the groundwork for mathematical concepts such as seriation and sequencing
- Engage in a purposeful, self-directed activity that fosters concentration
- Build problem-solving skills
- Build fine-motor skills and refine dexterity

"We shall walk together on this path of life, for all things are part of the universe and are connected with each other to form one whole unity."

—MARIA MONTESSORI

Materials:
- Sticks of varying lengths

Let's Do It!

1. Prepare the environment. Set up a relatively flat workspace, cleared up, with enough room for the child to arrange the sticks.

2. Gather sticks together. It's ideal to find sticks from the same tree so that the weight of wood is consistent, for the child to feel and explore in the different lengths and sizes (e.g., the longest stick is heavier in weight than the shortest stick). You should find ten sticks from about 10 cm to 100 cm long (3.9 in. to 39 in.). It doesn't need to be perfect, but you get the gist!

3. Introduce the concept. Invite the child to feel and explore the different lengths, emphasizing the concept of size.

4. Demonstrate how to arrange the sticks from the longest to the shortest, forming a linear sequence. Use clear and deliberate movements, using minimal words. Introduce the names of the rods by referring to them as "longest," "second longest," and so on. This helps lay the foundation for mathematical concepts like seriation.

5. Present the maze. Once the child is familiar with the sticks, introduce the maze by explaining that they will now use their skills to arrange the sticks in the correct order within the maze. Using slow, clear, and deliberate movements, model how to create the maze. Model your slow and intentional walk through the maze without bumping any sticks.

6. Invite exploration. Encourage the child to explore the maze independently. Let them handle the rods, arrange them, and navigate through the maze.

7. Encourage repetition. Encourage the child to repeat the activity multiple times if interested. Repetition fosters mastery and reinforces the concepts of size grading, spatial awareness, and sequencing.

8. Allow for creativity. Once the child is comfortable with the basic arrangement, encourage creativity. They can explore different patterns or designs within the maze, promoting imaginative thinking.

9. Conclude with respect. Respect the child's pace and interest. Conclude the activity when the child indicates they are finished, allowing for a sense of autonomy.

NATURE SCAVENGER HUNT

This is a simple, joyful, and educational experience that fosters a connection to nature. Adjust the difficulty of the scavenger hunt based on the age and interests of the children involved.

if

- The child is seeking something to do and in need of direction
- The child has an interest in observation and details

when

Ages two and up

then

Then offer this to:

- Encourage children to develop observation skills
- Boost cognitive development in categorizing and identifying objects based on specific criteria
- Refine fine-motor skills as children pick up, handle, and place objects in their collection boxes
- Promote problem-solving skills and critical thinking
- Connect children with nature, promoting environmental awareness and appreciation
- Provide a healthy dose of physical activity, contributing to overall well-being
- Support language development and vocabulary expansion

Materials:
- A box small enough to carry in little hands and big enough to collect some cool items
- A hand-drawn or printable scavenger hunt guide with words and images
- Magnifying glass (if available)

Let's Do It!

1. Choose a location. Decide where the scavenger hunt will take place, whether it's a local park, backyard, or nature trail.

2. Create a list. Develop a list of items for the kids to find in nature. Include a variety of things like leaves, rocks, flowers, or even specific colors.

3. Prepare materials. Provide each child with a small box or a bag to collect their treasures. Decorating the boxes beforehand can add an extra fun touch. Tape the list inside the box for ease of use.

4. Explain the rules. Gather the kids and explain the concept of the scavenger hunt. Emphasize the importance of staying safe, respecting nature, and sharing the adventure. Search only for already fallen leaves/flowers/pinecones/etc. to respect nature. Remind them to be gentle with nature and not to disturb plants or animals.

5. Collect treasures. As the kids find items, have them collect them in their boxes.

6. Explore creativity. Encourage creativity by allowing the kids to find items not on the list if they are interesting or beautiful. This adds a personal touch to their collections.

7. Gather and share. Once the hunt is over, gather together and give them a chance to share their treasures. This can be a fun and educational moment, discussing the different items they found.

8. Reflect and thank nature. Take a moment to reflect on the experience. Discuss what the kids enjoyed most and express gratitude for the beauty of nature. Consider concluding with a simple thank-you to the environment.

THE MIND TABLE

4+ y

Teach children about emotions and how to work through them using stuffed animals for storytelling. This activity engages children in understanding and managing their feelings in a playful and interactive way. Through the Mind Table, we help children understand that their feelings are an important part of who they are. We also give them a sense of control over emotions that can feel so big and pretty scary. It's such a helpful tool in raising emotionally intelligent kids!

if	when	then

If you notice:

- The child is experiencing conflicting emotions
- Signs of dysregulation more often
- A need for more emotional literacy (which is always good to work on!)

Ideal for children aged four and up

Then offer this to:

- Help children understand and manage their emotions
- Recognize that feelings are transient
- Empower children in the knowledge that they do have some control over their emotional responses

203

Materials:
- Four stuffed animals representing different emotions
- A table

Let's Do It!

1. To help visualize the Mind Table, we set up four stuffies, one in each seat at our kitchen table. One stuffed animal to represent each color zone, with you, the adult, at the head of the table, "hosting a meeting."

2. Begin by inviting the child to check out the meeting you're having with the stuffies and explain that each one represents your feelings; for example, brown bear is joy, elephant is sadness, bunny is anger, and crocodile is nervous.

3. Explain that everyone has these feelings inside them, and they're all perfectly normal. Continue to explain that you like to meet them at your Mind Table—a place in your mind where all emotions get a chance to share how they're feeling, and you, the owner of your feelings, can decide for how long each one runs the meeting.

4. You might say, "Thank you everyone for coming to our Mind Table meeting. I want to talk about how summer is ending. I'm having a lot of feelings about it and each of you can have a turn sharing, so that I can work through them. Would anyone like to share?"

5. Demonstrating: "Oh, Crocodile, you're saying you're worrying that school is starting again and you wonder about your new teacher and which friends will be there? Ugh, man—yeah, that's so hard! I hear you." Explain to the child, "We actually get to decide how long thoughts stay! I can say, 'Hello, Nervous, I acknowledge your feelings; I don't want to get stuck in them though. So I hear you and I'll see what I can find out about our new teacher! I bet I can find a picture of him and ask some friends what he's like. Thank you for sharing how you're feeling; you can sit back down now." This helps us (adults and kids) remember that we can honor our feelings, notice them, and let them pass by. We can then invite other feelings to share.

6. We can, and should, feel each feeling of our Mind Table, remembering that no feeling lasts forever, and we decide how long they stay.

7. This helps children get to a point where they can notice a feeling coming and say something like, "Hello, I hear you, Anger. You need to get out. I'll turn on some music and stomp my feelings out so you don't get stuck."

Storytelling and the use of stuffed animals or puppets to explore real life emotions is shown by research to be a low pressure, effective tool in emotional development.

"We see the figure of the child who stands before us with his arms held open, beckoning humanity to follow."

—DR. MARIA MONTESSORI, EDUCATION AND PEACE

reflection

Bringing our time together to a gentle close.

I'd love for you to reflect on what brought you here. Why were you drawn to the idea of becoming a more respectful, peaceful parent? What is it about this journey that touches your heart? Some are here, working hard to show up for their kids in ways they needed when they were younger. That might resonate with you. Others might be inspired by their amazing parents, aiming to pass on that joy once again. Or perhaps, you believe in nurturing kind, empathetic, strong individuals as a path to a more peaceful world. Maybe you simply sense there's a better way. Imagine if we all worked on ourselves as diligently as you are now—how wonderful the world would be!

I'm here because I want to raise children who will be kind to yours, who value peace, and feel empowered to take on the big adventure of life before them.

My "why" is written on a little note, tucked in my bedside drawer, where I pull it out after a long day. All it says is this:

"Why? To keep their beautiful, bright light shining."

Every child comes into this world full of light and love, hoping for and needing connection. And if there's nothing else we ever do, we can commit to nurturing, not dimming, that light.

So, I ask you, please write down your "why." Why do you want to embrace peaceful Montessori parenting? What drives you to dedicate yourself to this every day?

Please take with you a reminder that we're all still, and always will be, on a journey of learning. We're not just guiding our children, but also growing alongside them.

Thank you so much for spending this time with me.

All about being me

I am strong.
I am so loved.
I can do hard things.
I am smart.
I am kind.
My voice matters.
I am brave.
All of my feelings are valid.
I love being me.
I am beautiful—inside and out.
I am capable.
My heart is so big.
I am important.
I have great ideas.
I am proud of myself!

What to wear today

The Weather

Winter   Spring   Summer   Autumn

Routine cards

Breakfast

Morning Work

Outside

Music and Movement

Snack

Lunch

Nap

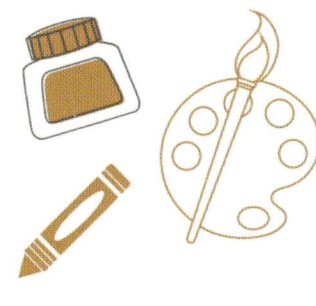

Art

Story Time

Bed Time

Shower

Brush Teeth and Hair

Dinner

Use Toilet

Pajamas

Quiet Time

Quality Time

Independent Work

How to brush my teeth

Wet My Toothbrush

Put Toothpaste On

Brush My Teeth

Scrub Up and Down

Scrub Side to Side

Parent Brushes For Me

Swish With Water

Spit Into The Sink

Clean Up Time

I am feeling

Happy

Calm

Mad

Sad

My calming tools

Breathe in. Breathe out.

Read a book.

Close my eyes.

Drink a glass of water.

Move my body.

Hug my stuffies.

Our family guidelines

resources

There is such incredible support in the Montessori and parenting worlds nowadays. Sometimes, it is just a bit hard to find. So, here are some of the books, people, and resources that I've learned from and share about every chance I get!

Books

1. *The Montessori Toddler* by Simone Davies—Provides strategies and insights into applying Montessori principles at home with toddlers, supporting independence and cooperation.

2. *Maria Montessori's Own Handbook* by Maria Montessori—This original guide by Montessori herself offers fundamental insights into her educational philosophy and methods, serving as a valuable tool for anyone interested in applying Montessori principles.

3. *The Awakened Family* by Dr. Shefali Tsabary—Challenges traditional parenting scripts and encourages parents to foster deep connections with their children.

4. *Peaceful Parent, Happy Kids* by Laura Markham—This book lays out a step-by-step approach to stop yelling and start connecting, fostering emotional communication between parents and children to solve common parenting issues.

5. *The Whole-Brain Child: 12 Revolutionary Strategies to Nurture Your Child's Developing Mind* by Daniel J. Siegel and Tina Payne Bryson—This book provides key strategies for fostering healthy brain development in children, offering practical insights to help parents turn challenging moments into opportunities for growth.

6. *The 5 Principles of Parenting: Your Essential Guide to Raising Good Humans* and podcast "Raising Good Humans," by Dr. Aliza Pressman provides research-based strategies and expert discussions to support effective and empathetic child-rearing. These resources are designed to help parents navigate the complexities of parenting with confidence, emphasizing respect, support, and understanding in family dynamics.

Blogs

Nicole Kavanaugh's Montessori blog, *The Kavanaugh Report* is a comprehensive resource that offers practical advice, creative Montessori-aligned activities, and insightful tips to help parents and educators effectively implement Montessori principles at home.
www.TheKavenaughReport.com
@NickAv25

Home and on the Way is a Montessori-focused blog by Ayelet, a Montessori mother, sharing insights and experiences from her family's journey with Montessori and respectful parenting at home and beyond. The blog offers practical Montessori-aligned activities, tips for setting up child-friendly spaces, travel, and guidance on integrating Montessori principles into everyday family life.
www.homeandontheway.com
@homeandontheway

Callie at *@Little.Farm.Montessori* is one of my favorite people and offers a comprehensive resource for families looking to integrate Montessori principles into their daily lives, offering online courses, mentorship, and hands-on learning experiences at a Montessori-inspired nature farm school to support holistic child development.
www.littlefarmmontessori.com

Blanca at *@wholechildhome* is a licensed professional counselor (LPC) and Montessori child herself, offers a Montessori-inspired resource that supports bilingual (English-Spanish) parenting through workshops, courses, and consultations, blending Montessori principles with positive discipline to nurture holistic child development at home.
www.wholechildhome.com

The Montessori Family UK blog, founded by Carine Robin, serves as an invaluable resource for parents and educators seeking to incorporate Montessori principles into their home environment.
www.themontessorifamily.com
@themontessorifamilyUK

Child of the Redwoods is a Montessori-focused blog and resource hub created by Aubrey Hargis, aimed at helping parents and caregivers implement the Montessori method at home. It offers a variety of Montessori homeschooling programs, community support, and resources to guide parents through early childhood education with a focus on understanding the Montessori philosophy and practical application.

www.childoftheredwoods.com
@childoftheredwoods

For more information on the study cited in "The Expectation Gap," page 59, see www.zerotothree.org/resource/parent-survey-reveals-expectation-gap-for-parents-of-young-children

Haley Turner's
Parenting with Intention Online Courses

1. Bestselling, *Parenting with Intention: 4 Week Early Years Course and Community*, offers a comprehensive deep dive guide to raising children using respectful and positive Montessori methods. The course is designed for parents of children aged one to six and covers discipline, emotional intelligence, setting up a Montessori home, and more, using research-backed, non-punitive methods. It provides practical tools and strategies to foster a peaceful home environment and enhance children's independence, cooperation, and emotional growth.

2. *Parenting with Intention: The First Year Course* for new and expecting parents to apply Montessori principles from birth to one year. The course provides self-guided videos and monthly community meetings, focusing on nurturing growth, respectful caregiving, secure attachment, and creating Montessori environments at home.

3. *Independent Play Course* is designed to help parents foster their child's independent play, an essential aspect of Montessori and RIE principles. The course offers practical steps for creating a supportive environment that enhances a child's capability to play independently. It includes modules on understanding the child's unique needs, setting up effective routines, and preparing physical spaces that encourage concentration and engagement.

4. *Raising Siblings with Intention Course*, offers parents strategies to foster a peaceful and supportive relationship among siblings from ages one to six. It provides a masterclass in sibling dynamics, covering topics from conflict resolution to empathy, grounded in research and best practices in parenting. The course includes lifetime access to materials, a printable workbook, and practical tools for implementing a nurturing and cooperative family environment.

1:1 and Small Group Parent Coaching

Haley offers Parent Coaching services that combine Montessori principles with conscious parenting techniques to offer personalized guidance tailored to each family's needs. These services focus on developing respectful, empathetic parenting practices that support a child's independence and emotional intelligence, aiming to create a nurturing and effective family environment.

acknowledgments

I am a firm believer that the art of noticing all the good in your life is one of the most valuable and impactful gifts to yourself, ever. One place to start seeing that good is in the people who make magic with and/or for you. There are many in my life who have contributed to each and every step of my career, this book, and, of course, my overall wellbeing. They deeply deserve their mentions here and I am grateful to know their names will live in this book for years to come!

Thank you so much beautiful little family for supporting me every step of the way. Dylan, your love is the backbone to my every wild and exciting idea. Knowing you'll rally alongside me, with a kiss on my forehead and a "you've got this" is everything to me. Our kids get to grow up seeing and feeling a love this big and I'll never take that for granted. And to my babies, not a moment goes by when I am not in awe of you. I will never forget the pride in your eyes when you told your friends that I wrote a book and helped other mommies and daddies. You've inspired every bit of the growth, healing, and work I've done as a mother, educator, and human being. You are the dreams I have always dreamt and my wishes come true.

Thank you to our support system for bringing this to life and caring for those dream babies while I write and create. Mom and Dad, you've always taught me that every goal is within reach, even if I've had some extra mountains to climb on the journey.

A special moment of gratitude to Angela Harrison—a therapist, mom to 3 of my favorite kids, and one of my dearest friends. My mentor in all things life, mothering, and navigating mental health. Thank you for giving me my first chance at work after brain surgery, when I was so lost and needed light. This book and my career as a whole would have never been possible without your introduction to this world of conscious parenting.

Joy Aquilino, you've been an incredible editor and such a light throughout this process. Thank you for honoring my vision along the way, while beautifully guiding us to make this book what it is today. Thank you to the entire Quarto/Quarry Team for giving this a chance!

To one of my favorite humans and the artist of our cover illustrations, Jessica Maher @j.maher_art, I am thankful every day to call you my sister-in-law and one of my very best friends. Thank you for helping me bring my ideas to life and making every step fun and full of love.

Last and far from least, thank you to my @Kindly.Haley community for making this happen. I am a published author because of *you*. Through every twist and turn, you have shown up for me and opened your hearts to learning and connecting in our Montessori and peaceful parenting online world. Everything I have been able to create is for you *and* because of you. You've given me such a gift and I will continue to be grateful for you every day. You are changing the world with every beautiful, authentic interaction and loving embrace as a parent and if no one has told you yet today, you're doing an amazing job.

about the author

Haley Turner is the creator behind the @Kindly.Haley Instagram account, Parenting with Intention Online Courses, and owner of The Kindly Co, a Montessori playgroup space for parent/child education and support. She is a mother, early childhood educator and parenting guide who has transitioned from teaching in a classroom to guiding parents online and in-person through their parenting journeys. Her approach integrates Montessori, RIE, Conscious Parenting, and Positive Discipline to provide parents with the tools for raising children in a connected, respectful, and empathetic manner. Haley's love for this work is evident in her online courses, which have reached thousands of parents globally, helping them to nurture kind, healthy, and resilient children.

At age 23, Haley underwent brain and spinal surgery for a rare condition called Chiari Malformation. She was then diagnosed with Ehlers Danlos Syndrome, a rare connective tissue disorder that has impacted her life significantly, causing unique physical health challenges. These lived experiences have led to her passion in making Montessori accessible to *all*. She believes that Montessori is meant to make life more joyful for the child, but also for the parent. Haley's goal is always to simplify the methodology and pair it with modern day research to encourage families to take small steps toward big goals of raising confident and capable kids in a holistic way.

For further learning and education check out Haley Turner's courses in the Resources section and at www.KindlyHaley.com.

219

index